Facets of the Future

CARMELITE MONASTERY
LIBRARY
SARANAC LAKE, N Y

Facets of the Future

Religious Life USA

Ruth McGoldrick, S.P. and Cassian J. Yuhaus, C.P., Editors

OUR SUNDAY VISITOR, Inc.

Nihil Obstat:
Rev. Lawrence Gollner
Censor Librorum

Imprimatur
✝ Leo A. Pursley, D.D.
Bishop of Fort Wayne-South Bend
March 29, 1976

The Nihil Obstat and Imprimatur are official declarations that a book or pamphlet is free of doctrinal or moral error. No implication is contained therein that those who have granted the Nihil Obstat or Imprimatur agree with the contents, opinions or statements expressed.

Copyright ©1976 by CARA ⊕ , Washington, D.C. 20005
All rights reserved.

ISBN: 0-87973-759-X
Library of Congress Catalog Card Number: 76-12194

Cover design: Vicky A. Reeves, C.H.M.

Published as a joint project by the *Sister Formation Conference*, the *Center for Applied Research in the Apostolate* and *Our Sunday Visitor, Inc.*

Printed and bound in the U.S.A. by
Our Sunday Visitor, Inc.
Noll Plaza
Huntington, Indiana 46750

759

A Prayer for Religious

Heavenly Father, we firmly believe that your son Jesus is in our midst, since he has said that where two or three are gathered together in his name, he will be present too.

You alone know what the future has in store for Religious life. But we believe that you will aid us by your grace, as we discuss what we think will be the course of Religious life in the future.

We pray humbly for the insights you wish us to have. Your divine grace can give us new insights about Religious life, which is suffering so much today because of tension, confusion and the anguish that troubles all of us.

Father, grant that all of us may reflect deeply on the challenges, the ideas, the suggestions herein presented and may we use them for the benefit of Religious life in the future.

We beg you, Father, to grant to the Religious of today and the future: deep faith, strong hope, and vibrant love. Grant that they may be deeply rooted in the theological and moral virtues. Actualize in all of us to a significant degree the gifts of the Spirit. Make us zealous in serving you and our neighbor.

We ask all this in the name of your son, Jesus and of the Holy Spirit.

Amen.

Most Rev. James J. Byrne, STD
Archbishop of Dubuque, Iowa
Chairman of the Liaison Committee of Bishops
for the Leadership Conference of Women
Religious

CARA Symposium: *The Future of Religious Life*
September 29, 1975

Futurism: A Cooperative Venture

In February of 1975 Sister Ruth McGoldrick, SP, Executive Director of the Sister Formation Conference, learned that the Center for Applied Research in the Apostolate (CARA) was to celebrate its tenth anniversary with a symposium on the "Future of the Religious Life." She and Reverend Cassian J. Yuhaus, CP, Chairman of the Religious Life Department of CARA, felt that it would be good for both organizations to cooperate since both were preparing programs concerned with the future of Religious life.

At its spring meeting, the SFC Leadership Board approved plans for its part of the Program: a bicentennial program entitled "Futureshop on Formation."

The brochure for the Futureshop set forth the board's objectives:

> The Futureshop will draw upon the experience, expertise, and intuitions of women Religious who are future-oriented. Such women have moved beyond a preoccupation with the past to new forms of cooperation and communion. They envision a more just and human society for our nation's third century; they intend to be in the midst of those creating it.

> The Futureshop has been designed as a "gathering of the resourceful." It will be a coming together of women who wish to share insights into the formative process and to explore approaches to initial and on-going formation.

> The initiative and foresight of pioneers in the Sister Formation Movement helped to prepare Sisters for the renewal. New challenges now beckon. Both the Church and society need the creativity and religious insight of Sisters who have the desire and the skills necessary to liberate hearts and structures.

7

No one can predict the future; but the resourceful do have intuitions about its shape. The Leadership Board of the Conference is confident that this "gathering of the resourceful" will be an important contribution to the bicentennial and to the future of the Religious life in the United States.

CARA's intent was not only to gather together experts to share their vision and their concern about the tomorrow of Religious institutes but also to announce a new research project that seeks to determine, with as much scientific accuracy as possible, the trends, the directions, and fears and hopes for the future of Religious life.

During the past decade, from the end of Vatican Council II until the present, CARA has been engaged by a large number of Religious institutes of women and men to assist them in a wide variety of projects, all directed toward a better understanding of Religious life today and a projection of that life into tomorrow. As one peers down the road ahead, the questions are many and pressing. These questions concern not only such important areas as formation, community, government and ministry, but go more deeply still. The concern is with the very basic theology of the Religious vocation and its multiple relationships in the Church, universal and local, and in civic, national and global society. The panelists at the CARA Symposium addressed themselves to some of these problems.

Over one hundred and twenty Religious registered for the one day CARA Symposium on the Future of the Religious Life. An additional one hundred and fifty Religious registered for the Futureshop, held at the Mercy Generalate in Bethesda, Maryland from September 28 through October 2, 1975. Futureshop participants from all parts of the United States and Canada included formation personnel, Religious and personnel development coordinators, community administrators, pastoral and campus ministers, associate vicars for Religious, and contemplatives.

The Futureshop opened on Sunday evening with an orientation and social. Futureshop participants joined the CARA participants on Monday for the symposium on the "Future of the Religious Life."

During the Futureshop, two general sessions were held: "Trends and Options" and "Futures Evolving from Past Identity and Experience." In the afternoons, the resource leaders initiated the four Dialogues which took place in small group sessions entitled: "Covenanting," "Emerging Ministries," "Learning Communities," and "Projected Tomorrows." The main dynamic in the small groups was the full sharing of ideas and opinions by the participants after a brief presentation by the resource leaders.

Two evening sessions were held. Sister Nadine Foley, OP, the coordinator of the Ordination Conference, spoke on ministry at the first session. She then answered questions about the Ordination Conference and the implications of this movement for formation. The next evening Reverend Gerard Weber presented the new multi-media Genesis II Program. Over fifty organizations sent material for display, and during the workshops futuristic films were shown.

On the final morning of the Futureshop, Sister Shawn Madigan, CSJ, highlighted nine value trends in her paper, "Projected Tomorrows and the Effects on Formation Today." Participants then brainstormed on consequences of these trends for tomorrow.

Although the time for dialogue was all too short, both the participants and program directors felt that the main objectives of the program had been realized. New hope and eagerness to plan for the future were engendered. Fresh ideas and leadership surfaced. Many of the participants decided on continuing the dialogues at home through mini-Futureshops to strengthen on-going formation programs. This also became a priority on both national and regional levels.

The Futureshop was certainly a symbol of the resourcefulness of women Religious during the 1975 International Women's Year. Other effects of the program can be seen in two significant actions taken by the SFC Leadership Board at its fall meeting immediately after the Futureshop.

The board voted to broaden the Conference's horizons and influence by opening up full membership to communities of Religious men and to non-canonical communities as well.

The name of SFC, the oldest Sisters' Conference, will be changed in 1976 to Religious Formation Conference.

The Leadership Board of SFC and the CARA staff are confident that the Futureshop and the Symposium were important contributions to the nation and to the future of Religious life in the United States. It was a hope-filled gathering of the resourceful in the nation's capital on the eve of the country's bicentennial.

Ruth McGoldrick, SP
Executive Director
Sister Formation Conference

Cassian J. Yuhaus, CP
Coordinator, Religious
Life Program: CARA
National Director,
Institute for Religious

Contents

Part I   The Future of the Religious Life: a CARA Symposium

The paradox and the conflict of the prophets are that they operate in the future while appearing to exist in the present. Or is it the prophets who are in the present and the hearers who are in the past? The conundrum is that we cannot tell. I, for one, prefer to believe that we are all in slightly different presents limited and/or extended by our own vision, values and style.

Pages on the Future
Elizabeth Ann Glysh, OSF

Part I: Introduction

The CARA Symposium attracted a large number of Religious men and women from every region in the country. In fact, every state except Alaska was represented. The panelists were chosen for their known expertise in various areas of Religious life and were representative of the various categories of the Religious life vocation: men and women Religious, apostolic and contemplative communities, clerical and non-clerical institutes.

In the collection of papers that follows, Margaret Brennan, IHM offers a reflection on the traditional ministries of women Religious vis-à-vis the demands of our present society and the significant developments in the understanding of the mission of the Church in contemporary society. Based on these new and renewing developments in the Church and society, Kathleen Keating, SSJ explores the very difficult question, "What kind of woman do we wish to come to Religious life in the future?" Her penetrating analysis raises an even more crucial question: "Are Religious communities of today really ready to accept the Religious woman of tomorrow?" While these questions are related to the urgent crisis of the role of women in the Church and society the issue is not the liberation of women, but really the liberation of all humankind. In the third presentation Mary Gehring, OCD, prayerfully and reflectively calls our attention to the movement toward renewal in the contemplative orders, with its present hindrances as well as its hopes and possibilities for the future.

Paul M. Boyle, CP, former President of the Conference of Major Superiors of Men, presents an optimistic view of the future. In reviewing the direction that the new code of canon law for Religious is assuming he sees greater emphasis on the role of Religious in the local and national churches as well as hopeful prospects for increased collaboration among Religious institutes on the national and international levels. Colman Coogan, FSC, while challenging the clerical model of the Church, investigates the future of the Brother in the Church with particular emphasis on the distinctive value of this vocation and its significance to the full concept of the Church as community in the midst of and one with the total human community.

In a very illuminating essay, "Response to Ministry and Change in the Future," James L. Connor, SJ compares the previous pre-Vatican II model of ministry with the contemporary model evolving from the new perception of the mission of the Church. He enumerates no less than fifteen reflections on the opportunities afforded Religious by the newly developing model of apostolic ministry.

1
Religious Life in the Light of Future Ministry

Margaret Brennan, IHM

It is very important to think about the future of Religious life in the United States, but I do not think it is yet possible even to sketch any simple, broad overview of what that will be. We can be sure, though, that its shape will inevitably be influenced and even structured to some extent — and in a very fundamental way — by the ministries to which we are called. I feel that today we are still very much "walking in the experience" of a search for a way to the future.

There is, however, an approach to such an overview. This is to recall and reflect on the traditional ministries of Religious, ministries to which very many still feel called. We can then observe the trends that are today operative in the world, in the Church, and in our communities. If we reflect seriously and hopefully on their meaning, perhaps we can, courageously, take those risks that call us to fruitful and meaningful action. In the course of this reflection we may be able to gain some insights at least into the future of Religious life in the United States.

Traditional Ministries

In the past many congregations of apostolic women were formed to supplement, strengthen, or overcome the weaknesses of our social structures. These important activities traditionally were concentrated in the areas of education and health care. In the large majority of instances, they were incorporated into or linked with the parochial and diocesan system. Today many schools and institutions are no longer "Catholic" in the old sense, but that is certainly no reason why Religious should give them up. The questions of overriding importance are not so much *why* but *how* should Religious be in education; and *who* should Religious be educating?

In recent years, the shift here has been to a pastoral ministry, to an accent on providing a religious education where others cannot or will not serve. And many Religious feel that they can no longer work in situations that do not call them forth in faith. But today's situation is not at all in contradiction to our traditional ministry. We shall always be called where education is, where the sick are, where the elderly are, where the destitute are — we shall always be called to whatever is marginal and scorned by our culture.

Trends in Religious Life Today

We are all feeling a continuing call to a deeper understanding of the Church's mission in the world today. This renewed concept of our mission is slowly emerging from the social theology of the Church of the Vatican Council. And Religious feel a continuing call, therefore, to meet and answer new needs.

At the same time we must realize that while Religious life as we have known it will not go on long into the future, nevertheless the greatest percentage, perhaps, of our membership have already defined themselves, have found themselves and feel they must serve out their lives as they are — and *cannot* profoundly change. We must realize this: that only a small percentage of Religious can truly live actively with these questions of change — and the majority must support them in their questioning.

This deeper understanding of the Church's mission, and this consequent widening of ministries, has had a profound effect on community life. There has been a general move away from monastic institutional structures and from monastical authority to situations that call for a more personal responsibility. And this has caused a crisis of community. How can we Religious permit — indeed, call forth — the personal, and yet not lose our sense of community? How can we accept plurality without losing our bond of community? We must learn to live with these questions.

We must discern where we experience the Spirit recreating and bringing new life. We must discover how the Spirit is forming us for Religious life 20 or 30 years from now.

Looked at from another point of view, we can call this question the challenge to develop an apostolic spirituality. We must understand that true Christian mysticism is a mysticism of commitment. We must understand that the contemplative and the apostolic Religious are united in the one same call to the experience of the Lord. We must realize that the sources of our Christian vision is the same: the experience of Jesus encountered in *prayer* and in our brother/sister — particularly the least . . . the wounded in our world. There is a great need for a much deeper internalization of this basic fact and dimension of the Religious life.

New Ministries and Community

At the Second Vatican Council, Sisters all over the world were urged to reexamine their lives in terms of the gospel, the charisms of their founder, and their mission in the Church and in the world. This call of the Council for renewal stands as the originating motivation for our changes. But once we began to reexamine our lives and our ministries we became more and more conscious of the demands that our society here in the United States places upon us — and of the gospel imperative to respond to these demands.

From a situation where most Sisters in this country taught in schools (mostly parochial) or ministered (and administered) in hospitals, we have moved towards one where Sisters are chaplains in hospitals, matrons in prisons, teachers of priests and seminarians, organizers of communities. There is no longer any single, basic "type" of Sister in the United States today. The only way "type" can be defined today is as a woman seeking to respond to the message of the Spirit spoken in a world where all categories are broken down and all definitions are being re-defined.

And this is the challenge to the Religious community. We must discover how to enable each Sister to make the most free and creative response to a human reality which invites both individual and common response. We must explore together — both the majority and the minority referred to earlier — how to integrate the varying moments of life-responses which trigger and reveal God's ever-active presence — in ministry, in prayer, and in community life.

The acceptance of this perspective may somewhat alter our present orientation and complicate some future developments in Religious life. We may find that our relationships with men, with women, and with married people may be different. Perhaps in the future the same Religious community will receive both men and women. And here we must consider the challenge of the present direction of the new code of canon law with its present definition of apostolic Religious life. If community follows mission, what does this say to us in terms of the meaning of community?

New Ministries, Church and Society

The pastoral questions emerging from the ministerial experience of active Religious women have made challengingly clear the pressing need to consider changes in canon law and the need to search for new theological formulations that will allow these women to serve the sacramental needs of Christians who invite and even call them to this exercise. Already, responsible biblical and theological opinion has reached some consensus that there are no clear biblical or theological objections to the ordination of women.

For some women, their nonadmission to orders (still maintained today in canon law) is an ambiguous statement of the inferiority of women Christians as Christians. To say, they argue, that any Christian is incapable *by nature* of receiving all of the sacraments — incapable *by nature* of full participation in the mystery of the Christ — is to say that there are two grades of Christians: complete and partial, first class and second class, superior and inferior, integral and defective ones.

But, on the practical level, even more immediately serious are the pastoral effects. Whole communities in the Church — not only in missionary countries, but in developed lands such as ours as well — are being denied a full sacramental life because of the shortage of ordained ministers. This is especially hampering to apostolic activity in the administering of the sacraments for the sick and the dying, notably among the destitute. We sometimes think of the situation in mission countries relative to the Eucharist, but I am speaking of the situation here in our highly urban United States, where it is an "intra-urban" as well as a rural problem.

This relationship between Sisters and the world we seek to serve has inevitably created a tension, at times, between experience and "traditional" law. All too frequently we have found ourselves in conflict with a code of canon law that has little in common with our lives and — regrettably — even less in common with the gospel imperative to which we seek to respond.

Will this tension and the resulting questioning of the validity of the present canon law for Religious (especially women) be reasonably resolved by some new, "more enlightened" codification? Perhaps, but the past ten years have shown us that we are only at the threshold of an important innovative experience. There is a grave danger in "freezing" what is really but a moment within a whole process of the evolution of Religious in the United States — an evolution begun by the Church, welcomed, urged forward and desperately needed by our society — and, hopefully, inspired by the gospel of Jesus Christ.

2

Religious Life, the Church, and Society: The Future Role of Women Religious

Kathleen Keating, SSJ

In these introductory remarks we have been asked to give a brief personal overview of the future of Religious life. I think I would like to raise a basic question which many Religious congregations have asked since renewal began. What kind of woman do we wish to come to Religious life in the future? There is no definitive answer, certainly, but the ideal is that she will have a deep faith-commitment, be mature enough to make a free and conscious decision, understand the call of the Religious woman to be a call to ministry in the mission of the Church to the world, is risk-oriented and does not possess security as a high-priority value, appreciates her gifts and is open to receive from others, and has a firm grasp upon her identity as a woman.

If this is the type of woman whom we wish to see responding to the call of Christ to become a Religious, then we have to ask if we are ready for her. If not, what must we become so that the vibrant, independent, loving, faith-filled woman will know that through Religious life she can use her God-given talents to carry out her baptismal promises to live a full Christian life? I am not saying that in the past we failed to attract strong and dedicated women. We can all list them, I am sure, by the dozens or even by the hundreds. However there is a difference now, and the future of Religious life must be viewed in the light of the changing role of women (in the United States) in Religious life, Church and society — the topic I have been requested to expand on.

The Changing Role of Women

First, I would like to view my perception of these changes which have occurred in the Religious life of women, and where these changes have brought us today. No analysis of the past position, structures, and modes of service which characterized the traditional life of Religious Sisters is needed here. We are aware of what has happened during the past ten years when most Religious congregations of women took seriously the mandate of Vatican II to examine our way of living, working, praying and governing. Perhaps at no time has history ever witnessed such a phenomenon whereby structures and lifestyles several hundred years old were turned upside down so rapidly and sometimes so abruptly. As we look back now the misunderstandings, confusions and polarizations should have been expected. Had the tensions and pains been anticipated we, perhaps, would never have entered the precipitous path on which we embarked.

Probably some wish now that the renewal process had been slower, picking up more of the pieces along the way rather than letting them fly off in so many different directions. But I would venture to say that not only were the changes necessary in order to make us more free to proclaim the gospel to the world, but also the very rapidity of the process served a salutary purpose. Moving from a posture of complacency to one of risk, from an attitude of unquestioning acceptance to one of continual quest, we certainly heightened our awareness of our vast potential and came closer to the Jesus of the gospel who had nowhere to lay his head.

As I review the past few years I am sometimes surprised that it was the shedding of the externals which apparently caused a great deal of tension. Yet it is understandable. In a life where so often the forms had become the substance, when some of the forms disappeared we were forced to deal with the question: what is our substance? "Internalization of values" we tend to call it. The reactions were mixed. For a variety of reasons many left Religious life, some clung more strongly to traditional ways, others used their newly found freedom to accommodate themselves to secular values, while others — and I believe the bulk of Sisters — entered seriously into the cross and resurrection contradiction of the reform movement. Thus, renewal has become literally a re-founding process whereby we, as Religious women, for the first time in the record of our existence, have the opportunity to make those decisions which will shape our lives for the future.

Presently, I believe that many Religious women, through their congregations or through other groups or as individuals, are in a reflective stage. We have had the courage to ask some fundamental questions — as fundamental as, should we survive? And if the answer returns that we are only surviving to maintain ourselves in existence, then there is no point in continuing. But if the question leads to others — survival for what, to be what, to do what? — then we can move on. Serious reflection is taking place on the apparently simple questions: as Religious women, what are we about? What should we be about? An attempt to answer these questions cannot be made apart from a consideration of the whole changing role of women in Church and society.

Whether it is a coincidence or an act of divine providence, the renewal of the life of Religious women occurred at the same time that many women in society as a whole were questioning their positions and roles. I do not think I have to review a whole history of the inequities and double standards from which women have suffered both in Church and society, and which the aware woman of today is attempting to change and overcome. The women's movement seeks equality of opportunity for women in all phases of life — economic, political, social, religious. Thus, the confluence of these two movements — the women's liberation movement in the broader society and the movement of women Religious to be the determiners of their own destiny — opens up to the Religious woman greater consciousness of the vast possibilities for the future of what she can do, be and become.

The changes for Religious women, of course, took place in a changing Church — a Church which once seemed (and sometimes still is) interested mainly in the maintenance of the status quo. However, the Church opened itself to the world with some serious questions about its own influence on the world. And perhaps the most recent and dramatic aspect of that attempt to penetrate society with Christian values came in the Statement of the

1971 Synod, which said that it appears that justice is a constitutive element of the Church. The implications of that statement are being felt by all of us, but as one who is on the inside and part of the movement in Religious congregations of women, I will say that Sisters, just as they took their own renewal to heart, are embracing the goal of social justice with sincerity, dedication and determination, and I hope, a willingness to learn from their mistakes.

Thus, the Religious woman as societal woman and ecclesial woman looks to the future with a new vision as she ponders: What shall we be about? She does not reflect in a vacuum but examines her roots — the gospel and the spirit of her founder or foundresses — and then she tries to read the signs of the times. I cannot predict the result of these reflections for every Sister or every Religious congregation of women, but given this present moment in history where liberation is seen as an essential aspect of the gospel message, and the Holy Spirit is moving the Church in the direction of social justice, most Religious women are contemplating the Christ who was sent "to bring the good news to the poor, to proclaim liberty to captives and to the blind new sight, and to set the downtrodden free."

Signs of the Times

A common pattern emerges, too, in the examination of our first foundations as Religious groups: that our communities were called into existence to respond to the needs of the people at a particular time. In the light of these reflections, she reads the signs of the times and the needs of the people and perceives the alienations and oppressions which exist in our society — not merely the domination of individuals over individuals but the dominations of systems which hold hundreds and thousands of people in one form of bondage or another. All of these things point to significant developments for the future of Religious women.

As women respond more to the radical message of the gospel that Jesus treated all persons equally and developed mutuality in his relationships with others, a new theology of person will emerge. As women feel called to a ministry of social justice, they will find in their own Church dramatic injustices in structure and attitudes which exclude them from the full use of their own talents and gifts. As women continue to use their creativity and initiative in entering a greater variety of ministries, their new vision of themselves and their potential will not allow them to perceive themselves or their sisters in limited roles.

As a Sister becomes more aware of her call to be a full participant in the mission of the Church, she will find that she has no choice but to seek full equality in all ministries, all decision-making roles, and all offices in the Church. It will become for her a gospel imperative. In short, if she is motivated by the holy desire to proclaim the good news, she herself must be a sign of the fulfillment of the promises of the gospel. It is important to note that other Christian women will be among those seeking full equality. However, as a Religious woman becomes more aware of the diaconal role which she has traditionally played in the Church, then fuller participation will be a natural next step. Also, if Religious life is to be viable for the future and attract the type of woman we mentioned earlier, we cannot say to her: we invite you to further the mission of the Church, but your role will be quite limited.

Another phase of the future upon which Religious women are reflecting and which will affect what they are about are the questions: What qualities and values will I bring to the new roles which can significantly alter the unjust systems in Church and society? What difference will I, as a woman, make in Church and society? Do I simply seek power for myself? Will I become simply another oppressor? Some aspects of the women's movement seem to indicate that women may want to become another dominating group. That is why it is very important that Religious women be about the business of heightening their own awareness of those gospel values with which they wish to imbue the world — the universal values of a desire for peace and social justice, the development of and enablement of all people to participate in decisions which affect their lives, a respect for our stewardship over the earth (i.e., care for the land, the sea and the air and all their products), and finally, the pursuit of the economic well-being of all people.

The primary quest of a Religious woman cannot be her own liberation but that of all humankind — the liberation of men as well as women from slavery to those attitudinal and behavioral norms which prevent us from becoming full persons. An implication of this last point is that through liberation those qualities which traditionally have been considered feminine — such as tenderness, sensitivity, healing, nurturance, gentleness — qualities which the world needs so badly, will be ever more present to society whether they are expressed through the male or the female.

From all this awareness of their potential and through their greater mobility, Religious women will continue to enter a greater variety of ministries, as is already the trend, ministries which will be directly pastoral or will involve her in positions which aim at systemic change. She will also remain in traditional ministries such as education and health care, but with a difference. Using justice criteria she will challenge institutions in their structures and operations.

Lifestyle is another aspect of life to which Sisters are giving much consideration. Whether Sisters will or should adopt a radical lifestyle of poverty, I cannot say. Our societal milieu and our personal upbringing may keep us from "pulling it off," so to speak. However, a Christian community which by its very existence proclaims resurrection must in some way take a prophetic stance and be counter-culture to the death-experiences of our present society, such as consumerism, materialism, competitiveness, excesses of wealth and poverty, isolation, ecological waste, and so on. Out of the present examination of poverty and our roots, a simplicity of lifestyle will develop, hopefully, which will make an attempt to operationalize in our everyday lives the justice values we so often talk about in larger terms. Our manner of recreation and celebration, our means of travel, our habits of eating and drinking, our attitude toward clothes and other personal possessions will communicate to ourselves and others that we are stewards and not possessors of the earth's resources, that risk is a gospel value, and that we have no right to an over abundant share of the goods of the world.

The Open Community

Also, for the Religious woman who takes renewal seriously, greater openness will characterize our communities. Perhaps this openness may take the form of women coming to share life with us only for a time; or those who will never live in community for a long period of time but will be associated with us in some way because we share common goals and objectives. It may be that mixed communities of married people and celibates will develop more fully. However, I cannot get caught up in forms. I do not know if they are important. What is important is that Religious women, true to their original charisms, will respond to needs and be open to those forms which will enable them to respond to the needs of others, and Religious communities will be places of refreshment, light and peace for themselves and others.

Whatever the forms of community some Religious now see as a particular need, the bonding with other women could include sharing lifestyles, ministering together, rallying around issues, coalescing organizations, or taking up the cause of those women whom society most neglects. The mutual goals which many women share indicate the necessity of support for each other, particularly as Religious women already have an organizational base and a sense of community with other women. In trying to bring about change in the Church it is of particular importance that we reach out and join hands with Catholic lay women so that they will not know an added pain of exclusion. Also, in view of our justice goals Religious women in the United States must examine themselves and their congregations on evidences of racism which have excluded so many minority groups from our midst, and move toward solidarity with the goals of our Black, Hispanic, native American and Oriental Sisters who have chosen Religious life.

There are many other aspects of the future, but I would like to conclude by saying that the greatest gift which we bring to the future is the heritage of the prayer-filled, dedicated lives and deep faith-commitment of those countless hundreds of women Religious who have preceded us. Without their example of prayerful active lives, we could never be at the point of moving into the future through these years of transition. Hopefully, like them we shall be contemplatives in action.

3

Toward the Future
of Contemplative Life

Mary Gehring, OCD

*The Lord God lives in whose presence I stand . . . with zeal have I
been zealous for the Lord God of hosts* (1 Kings 17:1; 19:10)

These words of Elijah the prophet have come to my mind over
and over again in recent months as I prayed and reflected on the
future of Religious life. "The Lord God *lives*, . . . with zeal have I
been zealous for the Lord God of hosts." Elijah declares Yahweh!
By his life he exemplifies what the prophet is in the Old Testament and heralds the prophet's role in the new dispensation:
that of being in the Lord, proclaiming a living God, a God who is
love, who incarnated himself in his son, Jesus, the Christ, and
gave new life through his Spirit, that all who believe in him might
have life.

I would like to divide my brief reflections on the future of
Religious contemplative life into three aspects: first, the basic
contemplative dimension in every person and therefore in all
forms of living the Christian commitment; second, my own experience and that of other contemplatives in recent years; and third,
hopes and possibilities for the future.

The Contemplative Dimension

We are called to life, to personhood, to be and become. As persons, we are endowed with the ability to reflect, to discern deeper

meanings in ourselves and in life. We can make decisions, be self-determining, increase our awareness of who we are as woman and as man. In our relatedness with others we come to experience what this means in all of life as it moves in time and space. Throughout history human beings have recognized that the choice of life involves the paradox of death and life: the mystery of suffering, anguish and death; the mystery of life, joy and fruitfulness. In the heart of every person there is an emptiness and a hunger and as Pascal said, "A vacuum that will be filled." We are restless until we rest in God, whether we call him/her God, the Absolute, the Source, the Center of our being, or by any other name or ideology.

As Christians our ultimate identity is found in his Person, in whom we live and move and have our being. In Christ Jesus we are ever becoming like the image of the Father's glory. As Christian prophets this is our mission, to be and become who we are called to be and to proclaim this good news by our lives, to witness to the Lord in the service of love. It is in this light, in this relationship that we are enabled to live the evangelical counsels and follow the Spirit in the Church and world today. We must experience the living God daily in the center of our being, in prayer and reflection, in the consciousness of being loved and in the radicalness of pure faith, in every person, friend, enemy, in all creation and in every event. Only then can we understand and freely enter into the anguish and death, confusion, alienation and quest for liberation that is in ourselves and every person today. Only then can we experience true *metanoia*, the healing of the diverse forces within ourselves, and be enabled to heal, to reconcile, to be loved and to truly love. Then we know in the biblical sense that the Lord God *lives* and our very life, our witness and our zeal flow from and are empowered by his life, his Spirit.

The Lord God *lives*. . . . This is the quest and the experience of the contemplative. It is my own experience, renewed continually by the power of God working in me, healing me, recreating me in mind and heart and body.

I believe this experience of God is inherent in genuine Christian life and vital to the future of all Religious life. I have also discovered that many of our problems and difficulties as contemplatives are sociological ones, and are being experienced by everyone, within and without the Church, culturally, nationally, and internationally. We are part of a sociological evolution, of a whole mutation that is taking place. While it is a journey into the unknown, the more I experience our God of salvation history working now, in me and in our time, the less fear and the more joy I have in being part of this whole level of consciousness and struggle for liberation in the truth of Jesus, the Christ.

There is much to be done. What has occurred I see as stepping stones in this process of greater and greater movement of the Spirit in what is yet to be.

In the search for the future of monasticism, we need to look at the past. Historically, monastic contemplative life has always been the quest for God. In the early Church, virgins lived simply and poorly; they were members of the local church. When men and women went into the deserts of Egypt and Palestine, their lifestyle became a school of prayer for the others who followed them for longer or shorter periods of time. Solitude and silence were requisites for the desert experience of God; however, these women and men were always considered laypersons in the Church. Their lives were marginal and they retained flexibility until the legislation of later ages.

In response to Vatican II and to the inner workings of the Spirit, contemplatives have been in the process with the rest of the Church of rediscovering the gospels, the charism of their order, and the call of the Spirit in them today. In my own life and community this has taken shape in a double movement: the positive affirmation of our life of prayer and its apostolic fruitfulness, and a greater consciousness of the needs and aspirations of our time, a realization of our part in the Church and world today.

This double movement has had several effects: the encouragement and growth of persons in being and becoming, the intensified living of solitude and eremitical life, and the deepening of relationships in a warm and genuine faith community. Through increased prayer and study we are in a gradual discernment process of what is truly evangelical and what is essential to Christianity and monasticism. For us Carmelites, this includes a clearer understanding of what is essential in our Teresian Carmelite charism and what is simply the reflection of the cultural mores of 16th century Spain.

Possibilities for the Future

In this age of dialogue and mutual upbuilding, we have benefited greatly through sharing with one another. The Association of Contemplative Sisters was begun in 1969 by 136 Sisters of different contemplative traditions in response to the felt need to work together. The prayer seminars and programs the Association has sponsored have been invaluable. Most beneficial have been the shared vision and hope, challenge and enrichment that collaboration has provided. This enrichment and collaboration, prayer and study have also been furthered by Carmelite Communities Associated, begun in 1970 and now comprising 19 Carmelite communities in this country. Each association developed from the vision and needs of the members and they are not patterned on the statutes of a federation.

In this brief sketch I will mention just two areas of concern. *Perfectae Caritatis* called all Religious to assume responsibility for their renewal in the Church. Because each contemplative monastery is autonomous, there have not been adequate means to implement this responsibility in world-wide orders. Final decisions are to be made by the Fathers General of the First Orders. Lack of communication and varied interpretations of enclosure laws have led to misunderstandings and polarization. It is hoped that contemplative women will be enabled and encouraged to fulfill their responsibility for their own renewal. We recognize that there must be a willingness to pray and discern together and that maturity, further study and training are needed.

The second area of concern I would like to touch on is the new canon law. Father Kevin O'Rourke's fine article in the January 1975 *Review for Religious* outlines the excellent principles and characteristics on which the section "Institutes of Perfection" was written. In general, the new canon law respects the equality, dignity and maturity of women as well as of men. However, these principles do not seem to be applied to contemplative nuns. We would like to see equal rights and privileges given to men and women living the same contemplative monastic life.

Along our journey in renewal we have been greatly helped by our apostolic Sisters, Brothers and lay persons, whose lives, experience and expertise have enriched and encouraged us. In receiving from others, and in the development of our own growth and fruition in our contemplative life, we have discovered that we have a gift to give and that others need and wish to receive our gift as we need theirs. We have realized increasingly that we are inserted in society just as contemplatives were in the early Church. We believe this is our rightful role as contemplative women today.

Practically speaking, Religious and lay persons have shared our contemplative life. In a limited way, we have also shared our contemplative monastic experience with Christians and persons of other beliefs. I honestly cannot articulate the profound Presence and joy, new life and solidarity I have known in those times of praying and sharing together. There is but one life in Jesus Christ. While we express this life in different ways, we need one another, and our lives are enriched by sharing our prayer-life. Truth is one. In Christ Jesus there is no longer slave or free, Jew or Greek, male or female. We experience the inner imperative to unity of all persons, races and creeds and the challenge to be freed of all that keeps us bound and divided, so that individually and together we may come to the fullness of Truth, the Truth that unites and makes us free. It is challenge that opens vistas for the future.

For all Religious, it seems to me, the one essential is Jesus Christ and the new life his Spirit is creating in us today. For contemplatives, the constants of monasticism will always remain: continual prayer, solitude, silence, joyful penance. We must be willing to let go of everything that is not helpful to these essentials and be open to whatever new forms prayerful discernment indicates. This involves risk, pain and death so that new life may arise. It necessitates faith in Christ Jesus and trust in his love and continuing presence in us, in his Church and world. It demands letting love cast out fear — fear that prevents us from entering into our deepest selves and fear that prevents opening ourselves to others and reaching out in love.

It seems to me that our journey in faith is taking us in several directions: an emphasis on evangelical simplicity and poverty; greater flexibility within the monastic structure; encouragement and fostering of new forms of living the contemplative life; greater awareness of and prayerful solidarity with the poor, the destitute and the oppressed and those who work for social justice and peace; and an openness to the contemplative experience in other religions that I have already mentioned.

Another direction in which the Spirit seems to be leading us (and I believe it is most important) is to the discovery of what constitutes an American monasticism: that is, the integration of our Teresian Carmelite life with our culture and time. We are a vital part of a transnational Church, a global village, a world-wide Carmel and monasticism; yet we are part of our country and our time with all its hopes, possibilities, struggles and problems. We cherish and continually seek to discover what is best and of the essence in our rich charism and tradition; at the same time, we belong to our culture as our founders belonged to theirs. As a faith community, we witness to "Jesus Christ, yesterday, today and the same forever," who says through his Spirit, "Behold I make all things new!" Therefore, we feel impelled to provide in radical simplicity the environment for true desert experiences to occur in our time, and to radiate the human face of Christ by mature, integrated, responsible lives, witnessing in the service of love.

The Lord God *lives*. . . . Glory be to him who can accomplish in us infinitely more than we can ask or imagine. The challenge is with us: Will we let the Spirit empower us anew each day and, through us, create the future?

4

The Future of Religious Life

Paul M. Boyle, CP

It is significant that this meeting is discussing the future of Religious life. Only a few short years ago we heard solemn and somber announcements of its demise. Less opinionated seers but no less lugubrious souls, conceding that death had not yet arrived, lamented that there was no future for Religious life. Crusading messiahs appeared assuring us that her or his insight was an absolute prerequisite for its survival, to say nothing of its vitality. Throughout all of these dirges, laments, denunciations and prognostications the *anawim* persevered in fidelity, in hope and in prayerful openness to whatever might be the will of the Spirit for them. The storm has died, winter has passed and the denouncers have departed. Spring is in our midst and we look with renewed joy and eager hope to discern the shape of the new flowering of Religious life.

Today even the more faint-hearted can see the tips of the new shoots; the fragrance of growth is in the air. Once again we are reminded that God's gifts are without repentance. The Spirit of God will always be in the future: faithful and inventive, creative, life-giving and guiding.

The new growth, the shoots from the new soil are too young to classify. There is a danger that our facile judgments will seek to impose an alien form on them, or provide them the kind of nourishment to become the sturdy tree we believe they ought to be — rather than the fragrant yet probably fragile blossom they are destined to be. With that warning as justification for my

36

timidity in describing the shape of things to come, let me begin by saying that a rebirth, a reflowering of Religious life is the one reality I see most clearly.

In all three of our worlds youth searches for meaning; they long for a mysticism, a spirituality. This quality is already apparent in our Religious communities, and will grow. Tomorrow's candidates will be more directly concerned with gospel values, they will seek a more evangelical life of faith and prayer.

To date, a large part of our effort at adaptation has been a process of acculturization. We have striven to make our communities contemporary, to make them authentically modern. We have adapted ourselves to our middle-class culture. I see Religious life tomorrow as an effort at counter-culture. Tomorrow's Religious will dramatize the kenotic aspect of Christian life, the emptying of oneself. Religious will be preoccupied with the poor, the neglected, those who have no voice. The apostolic Religious will seek to make her/his impact using only the weak and poor things of this world. The power of the cross will be made manifest to a consumer society.

Today we are preoccupied with managerial psychologists and specialists in group dynamics. In an effort to give splendid and striking expression to the beatitude of being poor in spirit, Religious of the future will search out possibilities of existence and decision beyond our present socio-cultural patterns of living.

One day has witnessed a critical re-evaluation and re-affirmation of the evangelical counsel of celibacy. Presently we are struggling to achieve a deeper understanding of the evangelical counsel of poverty, to see it as an effective apostolic instrument. I believe we are on the verge of experiencing the intimate and necessary connection between the emptying of Jesus and this first beatitude. Only when we have emptied ourselves like Jesus can we have that poverty of spirit which liberates and brings joy.

I have been requested to center my attention on the future of Religious life in the light of new developments in canon law; in the light of national and international conferences; and, finally, on the Religious life as related to the universal Church, the national Church and the local Church.

Developments in Canon Law

Basically, the changes which will be directly introduced by canon law are very few. The revised canon law for institutes professing the evangelical counsels will contain remarkably few specific prescriptions. Canon law will leave almost everything up to each institute to decide. The recurring refrain will be "to be decided by particular law." By removing practically all of the specific norms presently contained in the code, the revised law will foster a wide pluralism in institutes professing a life of the evangelical counsels. The revised law will urge "each institute to preserve its own doctrinal, spiritual and liturgical heritage."

The only legislation regarding the evangelical counsels will encourage each institute to express this reality in its own way. "Each institute, taking into account its particular nature and character, should determine in its particular law the manner in which the evangelical counsels of chastity, poverty and obedience should be observed in its own proper lifestyle."

I see one development in Church law, however, which will have a significant impact on Religious life. Accentuating the voluntary nature of a Religious vocation, the revised law will greatly simplify the process for any Religious who wishes to renounce her or his profession of the evangelical counsels. By the same token, the revised law will stress the importance of a life of the evangelical counsels that is a believable witness. Where this fundamental quality is clearly absent, the Religious community will be able to dismiss such a person. These two pieces of legislation will do much to improve the quality of our community life.

National Conferences

Despite strong reluctance and active resistance from Religious communities (and some bishops) the Sacred Congregation for Religious took the leadership in creating national conferences for Religious Superiors. The usefulness and impact of these national organizations will continue to grow. They will bring about closer collaboration between communities. We are already witnessing initial efforts in the Leadership Conference of Women Religious (LCWR) and the Conference of Major Superiors of Men (CMSM). Other collaborative or cooperative ventures, such as the

National Association of Women Religious (NAWR), the National Association of Religious Brothers (NARB), the National Center for Church Vocations (NCCV), and the United States Catholic Mission Council (USCMC), will flourish. A cooperative service in various areas of financial information and activity is in the process of being formed by Stewardship Services, Inc.

About a year ago *Businessweek* had a special issue on chief executive officers. Corporate CEOs now devote between 40 percent and 60 percent of their time and attention to civic and social concerns. A similar responsibility will rest on the chief executive officer in Religious communities, the Major Superior. In an active way, Major Superiors will represent their communities to the civic and ecclesial societies. Increasingly, also, the Major Superiors will present the needs and concerns of the Church and society to their fellow Religious. Superiors will seek to share information and awareness with their fellow Religious.

The membership of the Major Superior in these national organizations, her/his exposure to some of the pressing problems of our culture, their active participation on committees — all of this will influence the judgments and priorities of the Religious administrator. The Major Superior will seek to share this information and awareness with her/his fellow Religious. Searching efforts will be made to relate the role of their charism in response to these needs. Members of the community will become more keenly interested in making their contribution to these major concerns.

International Conferences

Perhaps one of the unique contributions of Religious will be in helping the local and national Church relate to the international scene. More than the average cleric, Religious often have close ties and personal experiences with people of other cultures. Members of our provinces or communities have frequently lived abroad for studies or apostolic service. Religious from different parts of the world gather in international chapters. Superiors and mission directors visit the community's mission activities. Our awareness of the universal Church and our sensitivity to the international dimension of decisions is strong. Sharing this global awareness can and, I believe, should be one of the contributions characteristic of Religious communities. Religious have surely been one of the significant factors in the growing awareness by American Catholics of the role of the United States in developing countries.

It seems to me that efforts toward fostering this awareness on the part of Religious will continue. Attendance at meetings of the Union of Superiors General (USG) and the International Union of Superiors General (IUSG) will be recognized as a normal part of a Superior General's role. International gatherings of Religious will seek to give a believable expression to our common concerns and universal fraternity — such as the Mexico City and Bogota meetings of representatives from national conferences in South, Central and North America.

The Sacred Congregation for Religious has not only encouraged such international cooperation but it has initiated similar discussions. In October, 1973 the Sacred Congregation for Religious hosted a meeting of the presidents of each of the National Conferences of Major Superiors. Moreover the Congregation for Religious has been meeting annually with the officers of some of the national conferences. This fraternal dialogue will, I believe, become a normal part of the harmonious relationship between Religious life and the Sacred Congregation for Religious. I would confidently expect that such gatherings of officers from national conferences will become more frequent in various regions of the world, especially for countries sharing a common language.

Local and National Church

We are already witnessing a wider spectrum of apostolic activity for Religious. This apostolic outreach will continue. This does not imply that communities will broaden their apostolates to include all services. Quite the contrary, some communities will return to their role of specialization. Whatever their particular apostolate, Religious will also manifest their concern and responsibility for other facets of Church life. As dedicated Christians they will bring their experience of the gospel to bear on the problems of their locale.

Religious will be ever more involved with the laity and clergy in apostolic works and other concerns of a broad nature. In a particular way, Religious women will become fully integrated into the parish ministry team. They will take their rightful place on

parish and diocesan councils. Religious Superiors will meet regularly with the bishop to plan together the apostolic thrust of the
diocese. Their awareness of the national and international scene
will contribute much to foster an awareness of mission in the local
church.

Because of the supra-diocesan nature of Religious institutes,
the participation of Religious in the life of the Church on a national level will always be strong. Many of their apostolates will
span dioceses.

If all of this sounds euphoric or utopian, let me append my
awareness that tensions, problems, misunderstandings and frustrations will continue. But the challenges to Religious life, the opportunities, will be stimulating. With the help of the inventive,
creative Spirit of God, the response of Religious will invigorate
the Church.

5

The Future of the Brother in the Church

Colman Coogan, FSC

A brief overview to brainstorm the next one hundred years:

- I believe there is undoubtedly a future for Religious community life, and in it the non-ordained male Religious will be as prominent as the priest-Religious of the present — possibly more so.

- Religious communities will continue to decrease in size for the next several years, but this will proceed at a slower rate than at the present. Their control of resources — financial, administrative, personnel — will diminish, but their flexibility and ability to influence will increase remarkably.

- A few existing communities will go out of existence, but new ones will be formed to meet the changing needs of the Church and society.

  The uniqueness of the basic charisms of the various communities will be seen more clearly. Many members of these Religious communities will assume critical leadership roles in the Roman Catholic communion, and together with their lay counterparts will be the change agents of the future.

- Among the new communities will be found married and unmarried persons, mixed groups (though not intermixed in common life), and even intercommunal (sects) groups for a time.

- For the most part we are still in the first generation of the renewal experience. Two or three generations of community life will be needed before these changes come about.

A significant number of former Religious of this generation will return to their communities, especially after having raised families, to take up the special work they left off years before.

In terms of time, we are still in the very early, cold days of the renewal springtime. In the words of Churchill, "This is not the end. It is not even the beginning of the end. But it is, perhaps, the end of the beginning."[1]

Evolution of the Religious Life

Justification for these assumptions about the future life are not predicated on precedents set in the Religious life of the past, but rather on what has been the nature and function of these communities in the history of the Old Testament and the Christian Church. In speaking about the various kinds of renewal already undergone by Christianity in its brief history, Christopher Dawson estimates that there have been five major upheavals, each of which was begun and ended by a major crisis, either governmental, dogmatic or natural.[2] Had Dawson lived much longer he would have realized that he was on the edge of still another such experience. Nevertheless, whether we accept the cyclic theory of Religious life evolution or merely accept a linear position of historical unfolding, we can see clearly the existence of radical renewal such as that which we are now experiencing. As persons of faith we must believe that all are attributable to the activity of the Spirit, a continuing revelation.

Karl Rahner in his treatment of Religious communities, *The Dynamic Element in the Church*, points out how these groups served as focal points producing tension in the Church which have had the effect of purifying both the hierarchical structure as well as the respective communities themselves.

The presence of specially gifted persons in the primitive Church is well described in Acts 2:4, I Corinthians 12:4-11, Romans 12:6, and Ephesians, 4:11. It is here that we learn of the existence of apostles, prophets, and teachers, together with those gifted in tongues, healing, miracles, government, and faith. Specifically, one might define these charisma as:

> gifts of the Spirit, ordained to the general good, bestowed for the welfare of the group and of the Church. The charismatic person is

moved by the Spirit in a manner that is over and above the gifts or-
dinarily received in the sacraments.[3]

Since the post-patristic period of Church history these charisms
have been institutionalized by founders in hundreds of Religious
communities. Not only have these men and women possessed the
faith in an extraordinary way, but they have coupled it with specific apostolic activity.

We know too that individual persons are endowed with special
gifts (both within as well as outside Religious communities), but
members of Religious institutes continue to carry out the primary
intention of their founders. They do this while at the same time
developing it according to the needs of the Church of each suc-
ceeding generation.[4]

While one becomes a member of a Religious community by virtue of consecration, subsequent roles frequently overshadow personal identity. I believe this has been particularly true of male
groups, where ordination to priesthood tended to separate
members of the same congregation rigidly, with the non-clerical
Religious being given the stereotype of the uneducated servant
who was permitted to join the community, but relegated to an inferior position. Only now, after many centuries, is this practice
dying out, and all members of a given group slowly are being
granted equal status.

By the fifteenth century new communities of men began to appear where membership was exclusively non-clerical. They were
most heavily involved in the education field but their role in the
Church is very often misunderstood. Once I heard them being
described as, "being like the Sisters except that they are men."
Try to live with that definition!

Quite naturally, the posture of the Religious Brother has tended to be defensive in a Church which has mistakenly allowed itself to be divided into clerical or non-clerical, with the former in
secure possession of an authority position throughout the centuries. However, progress is being made, as noted by the fact that
a Religious Brother was granted full credentials for the first time
at the last synod of the Church. Sisters enjoyed that status from
the first.

Church and Community Life

Religious community life has been a clearly defined mode of living the Christian life since the third century. In this way it has been a challenge and witness to the faithful. Quite frequently, trends running through the communities find their way into the larger community of the Church, and so it is well for us to be conscious of a role we carry.

Few words inside or outside of ecclesiastical literature run greater risk of becoming clichés than does that of "community." Taken from the Greek *koinonia*, it is best translated as "fellowshipping" and not as "fellowship," as it is most frequently rendered. It implies sharing, reciprocity. The Church is not an end but a means, a vehicle for the expression of Christ's love for his people; through it we find companionship along the way to him.

The vertical relationship of God and people of the Old Testament gave way in the person of Jesus to a companionship, a fellowshipping with the Father and the Spirit. This constituted the good news. Men were no longer slaves but brothers, as Paul says:

> The spirit you received is not the spirit of slaves . . .; it is the spirit of sons and makes us cry out, "Abba, Father!" The Spirit himself and our spirit bear united witness that we are children of God. . . . we are heirs as well: heirs of God and co-heirs with Christ.[5]

If there is any valid point to be garnered from the real suffering being experienced by Religious today it is the realization that they exist as communities of believers. To be such they must understand that fidelity requires an immediate, personal and affective response. As Erikson indicates, "fidelity is the ability to sustain loyalties freely pledged in spite of the inevitable contradictions of value systems."[6] Or again, as Bennis claims, "In a society in which all systems are tending to become temporary, partial and mobile, fidelity to other persons becomes almost the sole constant in life."[7]

Without an experience of fidelity one cannot live without threat to the self-structure, and without fidelity there is no elaboration of a faith. The "kingdom" of which the Church is sign and reality comes down to universal brotherhood and sisterhood.

One of the reasons for the failure of Christianity to achieve broth-

erhood was its neglect of sisterhood. Likewise, fraternity without sorority could never be joined to liberty and equality. The slip of the
metaphor was a massive fault not only in Christianity but in most
revolutions since then — an ideal of universal sister/brotherhood
has never been posited in history. It should therefore not be surpris-
ing that we have the kind of Religious organizations that we have.
    . . . Perhaps the sexes are more related than we think, and in the
renewal of the world they can come together as man and maid not
with false feelings or aversion but as brothers and sisters, as neighbors, and know each other as human beings.[8]

The Needs of a Renewed Church

There is no doubt that the Church — and with it, Religious communities — will have to pursue energetically many new directions. Greeley, with his *Agenda for Reform*, takes us from apolo-
getics to human relations. McBrien, in *Remaking the Church*,
lists thirteen specific areas of attack. Rahner has provided us with
the *Shape of the Church To Come*. And Dulles provides us with
five excellent *Models of the Church*. Finally, Moran has offered
us a new *Religious Body*. Each of these programs rests on a foundation of community renewal. As McBrien states: "By its relationship with Christ the Church is a kind of sacrament or sign of
intimate union with God and of the unity of all mankind."[9]

What happens in communities of men and women *today* will
condition much of what is to take place in the Church tomorrow.

What the Religious Brother Can Do

There is a unique role to be played by the Religious Brother in the
future Church. I would like to close by delineating that a bit
more.

First, I believe he must work collaboratively with the Religious
women to become with them the truly dynamic element in the
Church. A new image of personhood is needed and it can flourish
only in the context of human groupings where fidelity of persons
is a possibility. Only then can there be the trust, freedom, love
and respect spoken of in the New Testament.

Second, the clerical model of the Church needs to be challenged. Our richness lies in our fraternity and sorority as God's
children as we proclaim the Word. Whether one be priest or not
in this new light is not important so long as we see ourselves equal

to and at the service of our neighbor. For most Religious communities of priests this has not yet been achieved and will not be until they recognize themselves as community members first, priests secondarily.

Third, the foundation of Brothers' communities, as those of women did, helped to define the various ministries in the Church. It is time that the lay people in our society also realize themselves so divided: that they are not simply working people, but by grace and faith they minister to the body of Christ in their respective positions. This concept is little understood by the laity and needs to be explained and affirmed more widely.

Last, Religious Brothers have gone through their own identity crises and can lend compassionate support to all who are endeavoring to revise the structures which dominated them for too long. Faith, discernment, experimentation are the tools whereby this hope is to be brought into being, and while they are not unique to us our familiarity with their use is obviously something the world needs to know about.

References

1. Winston Churchill, "Of the Battle of Egypt," Mansion House, November 10, 1942.

2. Christopher Dawson, *The Historic Reality of Christian Culture* (Harper and Brothers, N.Y. 1960), p. 47.

3. *Sacramentum Mundi* (Herder, 1968), p. 282.

4. *New Ministries and Sense of Belonging*, Canadian Religious Conference, Number 20, pages 39-52.

5. Romans 8:14-17.

6. Eric Erikson, *Insight and Responsibility* (New York, 1964), p. 125.

7. Warren Bennis and P. E. Slater, *The Temporary Society* (New York 1968), p. 128.

8. Gabriel Moran, *Religious Body: Design for a New Reformation* (Seabury Press, 1974), p. 142.

9. Richard McBrien, *Church: The Continuing Quest* (Newman Press, New York, 1970), p. 77.

6

Response to Ministry and Change in the Future

James L. Connor, SJ

The basic form of Religious ministry has already been substantially altered over the past decade. I am thinking here particularly of the institutional works of Religious as, for instance, schools, colleges, hospitals, retreat houses, parishes, orphanages, and the like, which are staffed by members of a local Religious community. However, some of the following observations may be applicable as well to what are currently called "individual" ministries. (These remarks have only active Religious congregations in mind, since I am inadequately experienced to speak of the ministries of contemplative Religious.)

I shall attempt to describe the "before" and the "after" of this alteration in form of Religious ministry. This makes for conceptual tidiness and has the merit of highlighting differences. The living reality, however, is not nearly so clear-cut. In actual practice, individual Religious and different congregations are to be found at various points on a spectrum of transition from one form to the other. The value of this analysis will be the extent to which it enlightens the reader's own experience and helps him or her to plan more effectively for the future.

In saying that the form of Religious ministry has *already* been substantially altered from what it was a decade or so ago there is an assumption (conjecture?) implied. This assumption is that no such fundamental shift in emphasis will occur again in the near future, but that in the years ahead Religious will be giving fuller articulation and development to the model of ministry which currently prevails.

The two models, the "before" and the "after," might be named: (1) Ministry as extension of Religious community life (the "before") and (2) Ministry as collaboration in the world (the "after"). In each instance, the fundamental perspective from which ministry is viewed is quite different. Many of the same "ingredients" are to be found in both forms, but they are differently evaluated and organized.

We must, therefore, move through several steps: (1) a description of the "before" model from personal experience; (2) a brief statement of the new perspective; (3) the influence of Vatican II on this new perspective; (4) implications of this perspective for institutional Religious ministries; and (5) some reflections on the apostolic opportunities afforded by the current model.

The Previous Model

On the grounds that my own experience is as typical as it is personal and that illustration is more graphic than definition, I am presuming to tax the reader's forebearance by describing a Religious institutional ministry in which I once served.

In the early 1960s, I began teaching in a small, Jesuit liberal arts college. Dominating the fifteen acre campus from its elevated and central position was the Jesuit residence, the building which originally *was* the college when the Jesuits commuted from a center-city rectory. All top administrators and a large proportion of the teaching faculty were Jesuits. Curriculum and course offerings were established by the Jesuit provincial, not by the Dean or the President (who was also Religious Superior); and any change in academic or disciplinary life required provincial approval.

What most intrigued me, even then, was that all of us Jesuits felt very comfortable wearing our cassocks anywhere and everywhere on the campus. We wouldn't wear cassocks on the adjoining city streets, of course; but on the campus they were, we felt, quite appropriate. It was as if the whole campus was simply an extension of our residence. To be anywhere on the campus was to be "in our house."

On reflection in afteryears, I became convinced that this is ex-

actly what the campus was: an extension of the Jesuit residence —
not simply geographically, but psychologically, religiously, educationally, and every other way. We were running a kind of "con-
vent school" to which students were invited to come and share —
in a diminished form — the sort of Religious life which the Jesuits
themselves were living in an educational setting. Jesuit Religious
discipline and devotions, Jesuit ideals and practices, Jesuit feast
days and fasts, the educational courses and content suited to the
training of a prospective Jesuit priest — all of these were com-
mended to lay students, on the grounds that "what's good for us
is good for you." Mass attendance was required of the students on
certain days, the annual retreat was obligatory, the entire student
body was expected to attend the monthly First Friday liturgy in
honor of the Sacred Heart, May devotions were held daily in front
of a statue of Our Lady in the center of the campus, and so on.
The four years of Jesuit liberal arts education were patterned on
those of a Jesuit seminarian in his first years of training: two years
of the arts (poetry and rhetoric) followed by two years of systematic scholastic philosophy — though by 1960 some theology was
required of lay students and "majors" in professional and academic fields were available.

Further details could be elaborated, but it is the basic point
which is important: the student came to "live" with us and to
share in our Religious and academic way — all of this in a diminished and accommodated form. He (women were not in sight)
was invited to share in *our* experience and perceptions and values,
and thereby be formed in our, or the Ignatian, image. He came to
live in "our" world for a few short years before venturing forth
into "the" world, whose sinful enticements he would not only be
strong enough to resist, we hoped, but whose forces and currents
he would be educated enough to re-channel and transform for
good.

Of central importance was the fact that we Religious unilater-
ally established and controlled the total environment of our
"world." What was deemed inconsistent or harmful for us or our
students was simply denied entrance to that world, whether it was
persons, ideas, books, moral attitudes, films, movements, forms of
behavior, or whatever. It is because our ministry was an extension
of our Religious way of life at that time that we were able to exer-

cise this complete control over the entire shape and substance of the ministry.

To this kind of "world," then, one relatively isolated from "the" world, our students came for their education. And, in a great number of cases, grew in wisdom, age, and grace before God and man. It was a very good model for its time.

What has been said of Jesuit collegiate education of a decade and more ago roughly parallels, I think, the basic form of other Religious ministries, such as high schools, hospitals, grade schools, retreat houses, orphanages, and the like. It was a rather prevalent model and one in which Religious community life could not be — even mentally — disassociated from the apostolic ministry, since the latter was an extension of the former.

The New Perspective

There has been a radical shift in perspective upon Religious ministry. We no longer conceive ourselves as bringing students, patients, parishioners, retreatants, and the like into *our* world to share *our* experience. Rather, we conceive ourselves as entering into *their* world, to share in *their* experiences, and thereby share ourselves and the gospel with them. We feel a calling to be with God's people, where *they* are, experiencing their joys and sufferings in poverty and insecurity. We have a growing conviction that our place is very much in the world where economic, political, ideological, and social forces are shaping for the future the world in which Christ is ever laboring to be born anew.

This is a profound change of focus on Religious ministry. In a sense, the emphasis has shifted inside-out.

It is partially this shift of focus which has induced some Religious to leave corporate institutional apostolates in order to live and identify more immediately with lay people. They feel that even in a revised form traditional, institutional works block apostolic access to the "real" world and its needs. This accounts, too, for the emergence of smaller, more "open" Religious communities, situated in ordinary neighborhoods. Lay dress on the part of Religious is another effort to symbolize and realize closer solidarity with the laity. The renewed use of family names by women Religious also emphasizes unity with others in the human family. Growing political and social involvement by Religious both symbolizes and expresses a deeply felt desire to take a responsible part in those movements which affect them in common with their fellow citizens. The new effort, then, is to stress communality with non-Religious, presence and participation in the world, and solidarity with the human family, as the *locus* and focus of ministry. Rather than, "Come, be with us," the new emphasis says, "Let us be with you."

Institutional Religious ministries like schools and hospitals face special difficulties in finding appropriate forms to express this new perspective without losing their identity and proper purpose. Something will be said of this below, but first a brief description of the influence which Vatican II has had on the revision of Religious ministry might put subsequent discussion in sharper focus.

The Influence of Vatican II

Ministerial form and function rest ultimately on some perception or motivating model of Christ's mission to the world, for every apostle is called to follow Christ on his mission to evangelize the world. It is the rare apostle who personally thinks through thoroughly the "model" out of which his or her apostolic performance emerges, preferring rather to operate unquestioningly out of what seems to be the prevalent self-understanding of the contemporary Church.

Models of Christ's relationship to and therefore mission in the world have varied in their emphases — even in magisterial teaching — over the eras of the Church's life. The issue is sometimes put in terms of "Christ and culture." The same basic issue can be seen in terms of Church/world, or sacred/profane, eternity/time, divine/human, heaven/earth, transcendent/immanent, or the like. Fundamentally, it is our human effort to understand and live out the mystery of the Incarnation: the becoming-man of God in the world. The mystery, of course, is inexhaustible; and our understanding of it unfolds gradually generation by generation under the guidance of the Spirit who, we believe, attracts each generation by inner light and external events (the "signs of the times") to appropriate for itself what is most conducive for the furtherance of Christ's contemporary mission in the world.

The Vatican Council II set itself the precise task of discerning what, in our own era, the Spirit was revealing to us about the mys-

tery of Christ and the mission of the Church. The fruits of this discernment are to be found most notably in the conciliar documents
Lumen Gentium and *Gaudium et Spes*. And no one reading these
documents with an open mind can fail to find a striking revision
of emphasis in comparison with earlier conciliar statements of the
Church's self-understanding in its mission to the world.

Most responsible, perhaps, for the Church's revised self-per-
ception was the Conciliar Fathers' view of the *world*. While realistically acknowledging its deficiencies and sinfulness, Vatican II
sees the world and the whole human family as the object of
Christ's living and redeeming love. It sees the world as created in
Christ, in whom all things that are have their being. It taught that
it is the image of God in all persons which ultimately grounds
their inalienable dignity and their right to just and charitable respect. It recognized the presence of Christ and his Spirit in those
of other faiths and even in non-believers of good will.

Within this context, Vatican II recognized the indispensability
of dialogue among and between those of the Catholic Church and
all other persons in service of the fullness of Truth and of the integral building-up of the whole Christ in the human family. The
Church's role is to work in harmonious collaboration with others,
bringing to them its own life and tradition and truth as a light in
which their own strivings stand revealed in deeper truth. The
Council also confessed to sinfulness and deficiency within the
Church and saw that its own growth in holiness needs as complement the cooperative efforts of others.

Above all, the Vatican Council saw that for the efficiency of its
own mission the Church must be *in* the world and listen attentively to others and to the needs of the world, reading the signs of
the times through which Christ speaks no less than through the
scriptures and tradition. Presence, dialogue, collaboration, sincerity of service, trust and respect for all others, solidarity with a suffering world, openness to be influenced by other perspectives —
all of these are relatively new ingredients in the Church's most
recent self-understanding. They become formative features in a
contemporary "model" of the Church/world mystery of Incarnation, and it is out of this model that the Church's mission to our
present world emerges.

In its brevity, this summary can be no more than suggestive.

Moreover, it is admittedly selective in emphasis. It should suffice, however, to indicate how Vatican II's new perception of the Church's mission has necessarily and deeply influenced a revision of the former model of mission on the part of Religious congregations.

The New Emphasis and Institutional Ministries

It is in relatively large, institutional ministries of Religious that this shift of emphasis is most difficult to assimilate. Institutions, whether Religious or not, have a life of their own which fosters both identity and insularity. They respond to change slowly — even sluggishly. But institutions have been changed profoundly in the past decade. Very few, if any, institutional Religious ministries are modeled on the "extension of Religious community" form today. Of this all Religious are aware — some painfully so.

A review of some elements in this transition might be in order before concluding with some observations about the apostolic opportunities inherent in our present situation.

In an effort to understand and explain the very changed circumstances of Religious ministry today, as compared with a decade or so ago, some would contend that Religious Superiors simply abdicated their rightful role of leadership in the governance and control of particular works. Superiors "sold out" their communities by "giving away" a work to others through a transference of directive control and sometimes of legal ownership. This misguided permissiveness eroded and eventually destroyed the totally institutionalized environment which had given shape and substance to the apostolate for generations. The Religious community, therefore, lost its very *raison d'être* for service in this (now) "secularized" work. The alienation which was originally one of control and ownership has now become deeply personal in the confused attitudes and hurting hearts of individual Religious. Religious Superiors have themselves to blame, then, for the emergence of fundamental questions about Religious identity and mission. So this position goes.

It may very well be that some Religious Superiors moved too far too quickly down a road whose destination was not clearly enough perceived. There may also have been other failures in Religious leadership during this era, particularly in the area of caring personally and educationally for members of a community. But be that as it may, the position as such is an obvious over-simplification.

Other Religious very much appreciated and promoted the evolution from the previous model to the current one for a variety of reasons, some of which reflect the emphases of Vatican II. The "extension of community" model seemed to close the world out and the Religious in upon themselves too much, with the result that the needs of those served set the "agenda" less than the preferences and predilections of those serving. Ministry was missing its mark, and on either side of the "gap" both servers and servees grew restive.

Among the most important factors, however, in the dissolution of the former model was the introduction of many more lay persons into the work of Religious. When laity were few in number and submitted to the direction set by the Religious community, the previous model remained intact; but as their numbers, responsibility, and influence grew, the work could no longer be or be understood as an extension of the Religious community and its life. The work assumed an existence of its own over which Religious now simply shared responsibility with many — sometimes more — others.

The introduction of lay persons into the works originated by Religious was not solely, or perhaps even principally, a result of dwindling numbers of Religious. Rather, it was a choice made in view of recognized need and anticipated improvement of the work.

In a world increasingly more complex, there was need of expert advice about finances, management, development, and the like, for which temperament and experience had left most Religious unprepared. With the knowledge explosion and the advance of technology, whole areas of service were opened for a Religious apostolate; but realization of this potential required specialized training not regularly found with a congregation. Motivated by a praiseworthy desire to serve a larger clientele, many works expanded in size and diversity more rapidly than Religious could be attracted and trained to staff them. Finally, the experience, the spirituality, and the perspectives of lay persons complemented those of the Religious and gave a new dimension to the work in which each shared.

The coincidence of this movement with the emphases of Vatican II are apparent. Religious ministry came into much closer dialogue with the "world" and has inevitably been influenced by it. Collaboration with others has replaced a unilateral determination of goals and environment. A plurality of complementary perspectives prevails. The concrete realizations of this model do and must vary according to local circumstances, past history, current personnel, and the like. Each, however, is an instance of the same basic model, namely, "collaboration in the world." I would now like to offer a few relatively disconnected reflections about the apostolic opportunities afforded by this model.

Reflections on the Contemporary Ministerial Model

1.   It would seem important for Religious to accept the present situation gracefully, to ponder it carefully, to understand its potential strengths and liabilities, and to plan how to maximize the former and minimize the latter. Little can be gained from regretting the passing of a bygone era.

2.   Special thought needs to be given to the apostolic opportunity built into the very process of collaborating with lay peers in our works. Too often we restrict our attention exclusively to our "clientele" (for instance, students, patients, or retreatants) and regard our work and planning with lay collaborators as a negligible means to the real end. Actually, our greatest spiritual influence might well be upon those with whom we serve collaboratively; and, therefore, collaboration itself should be considered as an essential dimension of our apostolate.

3.   What may most influence our lay colleagues is the very example of our struggling sincerely along with them to seek and find where Christ is leading us and what form he desires our work to take. Such an effort to find the way will be more spiritually influential (and certainly more realistic) than the impression that we already possess a "grand plan" but simply lack a method to implement it.

4.   Central to this effort will be our desire to listen to lay collaborators and others in order to learn from them, to trust in their good will and sincerity, to encourage and praise their initiatives,

and to support them when they are discouraged. We exemplify thereby the poverty and charity proper to our Religious vocation because it is clear that, like Christ, we come not to be served but to serve.

5.   How to be deathly in earnest about the value of one's contribution, making every effort to see that it is understood and found acceptable and, at the same time, not to have or project self-interest, defensiveness, possessiveness, resentment, insecurity, contentiousness, and the like is an art which Religious are learning gradually. For most Religious, coming as we do out of a hierarchically authoritarian past, the give-and-take of a genuinely collaborative process in a pluralistic context is a relatively new and unfamiliar experience. How to influence, to argue, to persuade, to be willing to work for compromise, to be ready for the rejection of one's proposals — these are not simply techniques in the participatory process; they are sanctifying experiences for Religious. What angers and humiliates us most is probably where God is trying to teach us most.

6.   Religious works can survive and prosper as apostolic (within the originating congregation's spirit) only if lay collaborators come to share this apostolic spirit. Communication of this spirit, then, should be the principal concern of Religious. It is shared much more effectively through the *example* of the way Religious live out that spirit in the collaborative context than through verbal explanation. We have to be seen *doing* what we are called to *be*.

7.   Religious should welcome the fact that they have been freed from the grinding burden of exclusive responsibility for the management and funding of apostolic works. Now they have the time and opportunity to contribute what, by vocation and experience, they are best disposed to share for the benefit of the work and those with whom they collaborate: the life of the gospel, knowledge of the Church's teaching, the art of prayer, and the practice of spiritual discernment for discovering the Spirit's guidance.

8.   In a world given to illusionment, cynicism, discouragement, and indecision, nothing is more arresting than peace and joy based on confident faith in God's providence. To be able to invest oneself seriously into the confusion, conflicts, and unre-

solved problems of one's situation and simultaneously to retain one's joyful hope and peace is a gift of God and a great witness to the gospel power. Our current apostolic situation offers full opportunity to manifest this grace to others and give them strength.

9.   Peace gives freedom for very hard work. Now that Religious no longer "own" or "control" apostolic institutions, their hard work can the more easily be recognized as selfless and disinterested. Their service clearly witnesses to the poor Christ, who was motivated solely by concern for the good of others.

10.   Since the work is now much more open to a variety of "worldly" influences, Religious are daily in more direct touch with the trends, ideas, and issues which are alive in the world at large. This is continually educative for the Religious and provides a more realistic context for prayer and spiritual choices. It enables Religious to appreciate the pressures and opportunities which their lay colleagues face. This is especially so if Religious live in ordinary middle- or lower-class neighborhoods.

11.   As Religious experience more regularly and intensively the social, economic, and political movements of contemporary life, they are naturally awakened to a keener sense of their own responsibility for helping to shape the structures within which they and their neighbors live. In the process, they are drawn closer to their neighbors by collaborating with them as fellow citizens. This experience, in turn, inevitably flows over into their apostolic ministry, giving it a more realistic focus and tone.

12.   Social experience draws a Religious community's attention to the pluralism of views and convictions, not only in the world at large, but in the community itself. The world needs to see examples of persons who can live harmoniously even in disagreement on issues. What makes us one is our faith in God and respectful trust in one another, not a monolithic uniformity on particular issues. As long as our position on issues is not motivated by selfishness and as long as our unity is centered in God, harmony can prevail amid disagreement. This can be painful, but it is a rich opportunity for growth and witness.

13.   This new form of collaborative apostolic ministry is having an inevitable influence on the forms and style of Religious community life. What community should be now is not nearly so clear as in the previous model. Most communities are searching

their way. The challenge is to find a model which retains all of the desirable values instead of eliminating some for the sake of ti- diness and temporary "peace." For instance, privacy and openness are in contention, but *both* need to be maintained. Community apostolic purpose, on the one hand, and the varied apostolic reponsibilities of its members, on the other, might seem to be on collision courses; but *both* need to be retained. And so with other contending values, each of which can be enriching for the other and for the total quality of community life.

14.   The concrete "strands" in the collaborative relationship which a Religious community enjoys with the institutional work in which it serves will very much shape the style of community life. Around this relationship between community and work, the other dimensions of community life can be built up. This rela- tionship is of overriding influence on the style of community life because *collaboration* is the very *raison d'être* of a contemporary Religious community. That is why we have called it the current model of ministry. What does "collaboration" look like corporate- ly (i.e., for a whole community)? This is a key question for Reli- gious today.

15.   Imagery helps the understanding and development of models, and perhaps an appropriate image of our current minis- terial stance is that of "leaven in the loaf." The leaven is little. It loses itself in the loaf and yet continues to exercise its distinctive and irreplaceable influence on the whole. It "dies" to itself that the loaf might rise. It is the loaf, finally, which is important. It is different but not distinct from the loaf. It works from within, quietly, permeating through and through.

These reflections are hardly profound or original. Their value may be as "pump-primers," stimulating the reader to his or her own insights into the apostolic opportunities which contemporary ministry has offered us. It is a work of looking and seeing, of be- lieving and accepting, of dreaming and planning, of trying and erring — and of hoping with confidence that God will surely lead us to be with Christ as his co-laborers in the style of his mission today.

Part II   Futureshop on Formation

A Christian is only a Christian when she refuses to allow herself or any-one else to settle into a comfortable rest. She remains dissatisfied with the status quo. And she believes that she has an essential role to play in the realization of the new world to come . . . she keeps saying to everyone she meets that the good news of the Kingdom has to be proclaimed to the whole world and witnessed to all nations (Mt. 24:13). . . . She is irritated by satisfaction and self-content in herself as well as in others since she knows with an unshakable certainty, that something great is coming of which she has already seen the first rays of light.

—Henri J. M. Nouwen *(adapted)*

A Dialogue on Covenanting

To speak of covenanting and commitment is to speak of fidelity and relationships. The first article in this section discusses commitment in a
changing world. In it, Sister Doris Gottemoeller shares her own insights
as well as the insights of a seminar group which studied the elements of
permanency. Sister Kathleen Uhler next considers the necessary connection between Religious life and permanent commitment. She believes
that whatever is necessary and good for the fulfillment of the individual
person is required for similar reasons for the fulfillment of the corporate
person.

Sister E. Nancy McAuley, in highlighting the results of her own research on the vows as they are presently understood and experienced by a
typical group of women Religious, raises important questions about the
future of commitment and the vows. Sister Karen Gosser, a young Religious, relates her own understanding of Jesus' call and commitment, and
the implications of this for her own future and that of her community.
Sister Margaret Mary Modde presents a series of questions that stem
from her own work on the NSVC study on "Why Women Leave Religious Communities."

Sister Bernadette Casey and Sister Vilma Seelaus, experienced novice
directors, address themselves to practical and innovative ways of getting
to the heart of the initial formation process. Sister Ann Heilman and
Sister Maria Gatza speak of new shapes in on-going fidelity. Sister Maria
shares with us her experience and that of her community with Sisters who
are transferring from one community to another. Sister Ann calls attention to another phenomenon — the rapid growth of the largest "non-
canonical" community in the United States.

7

Commitment in a Changing World

Doris Gottemoeller, RSM

It is one of the paradoxes of our times that the act of promising —
even promising "for life" — should persist in the face of ever-
accelerating change in the political, social, and cultural orders.
The constant flux and impermanence of modern life affects not
only our environment, but also our very selves . . . causing us to
doubt, at times, the very possibility of pledging our fidelity to an
idea or to an ideal or to another person, since we are not sure that
we will be essentially the same person who made the commitment
after some time has passed. And yet, in spite of this, persons do
continue to make commitments, and in many cases to live them
out faithfully for a lifetime.

In order to understand the phenomenon of commitment more
fully, as well as the contemporary challenges to it, the Sisters of
Mercy of the Union undertook a study of the element of permanency in Religious commitment. The study, inaugurated in the
fall of 1973, followed a seminar format. After some months of preliminary reading, the twelve participants gathered for a weekend
of reflection and discussion together, and the taped record of
these discussions was edited into a pamphlet entitled, "Commitment in a Changing World." The following paragraphs summarize some of the highlights of the study.

The Present Challenges to Commitment

Objections to the possibility of lifetime commitment take many
forms. For example, a promise to love someone forever threatens

to lock one's feelings into rigidity or duty and thus to destroy them, or at least to set the stage for possible hypocrisy later on, when love has waned. Some persons challenge the possibility of perpetual commitment because they have subscribed to the "protean man concept," an image popularized by sociologist Robert Lifton. This theory of man views him as constantly changing from one commitment to another without any continuity — like the mythical god Proteus who constantly changed shapes in order to conceal his identity.

Others, who do not subscribe to this concept, still experience themselves as fragmented, without a sufficiently clear self-identity to make a deeply-felt and enduring commitment. Some shun commitment because they expect it to reduce their freedom; others because they believe human persons are too imprisoned by their culture to aspire to commitment. The fear of not being able to sustain the inevitable darkness and dryness which is one stage of an on-going commitment deters some. When our culture invites us to strive for a state of constant positive feeling, a "resurrection" experience without any "crucifixion," the difficulty in commitment seems intolerable. Finally, over-commitment at an earlier stage in one's life may bring on an "energy crisis" and consequent waning of commitment later.

Commitment and Human Desire

While there are persons who seem to remain non-committed, we sense that there is something in our experience of human life that makes most people want to make a commitment, even *need* to make one.

On the one hand, the desire may stem from our experience of being weak and fragmented and sinful. We want to love with our whole mind and heart and strength, but we know that we are not yet whole. We learn to be faithful, and so we give our word to the one we love. We gather up our whole life and our future and place it in affirmation of what we love, the right to call to us when our love falters and to strengthen us by that call. On the other hand, the desire for commitment may arise in us when we experience a prior call to it: we feel ourselves awakened in love for someone who seems worthy of our commitment, whose lovableness calls to our love and freedom.

On a higher level, God reveals to us his beauty and lovableness and faithfulness to us, and in that revelation is a call to a response. There is a message in that revelation that we will be somehow enabled by his gift, his grace, to respond to him with fidelity in unconditional love. Furthermore, although we may fear death through commitment (since we all know persons whose commitment has soured them and made them joyless), we also fear the kind of death that comes from non-commitment.

If there is danger that passion (devotion, power of feeling, emotion) will die in the process of commitment, so there is danger that without commitment passion will be wasted, diffused in a superficial search for an intimacy that cannot always be had in commitment, but can never be had without it.

Commitment Transcends Time

The relationship of time to commitment is highlighted by the evidence of changes in commitment and by our desire to give some interpretation of human duration and change. Only if our understanding of personal selfhood implies some kind of continuity of the self which perdures throughout the profound changes which occur over a lifetime, can we be held responsible for commitments made in the past.

It must be admitted, however, that some commitment changes may be justified. There are situations where, for example, it becomes impossible to keep a commitment, where a prior commitment conflicts with a later one, or where a given commitment deepens into another which fulfills it but goes beyond it. While admitting that a person can in good faith discern a call to change a commitment, it is also important to affirm that not every difficulty experienced (even terrible suffering, at times) signifies a need for a change or a justification of change. Viewing commitment as a way to integration and to wholeness enables us to understand development and growth within it. While a certain initial level of maturity is needed to make it wisely, one need not expect to be a fully integrated person at the outset.

In some sense, commitment transcends time: when we say "forever," we mean "I will not let the conditions of time or the circumstances at the level of duration erode that which I now say about myself to you." But in another sense, commitment is radically temporal. By committing oneself, one steps into a relationship which he or she expects to live-out in time. Although both partners will surely change and the relationship will change too, it will not change into non-relation. In that evolving relationship the negatives of commitment, darkness and dryness, will have to be built into the life process. In time, we learn how to nurture our commitments and how to integrate both the light and the shadow within them.

The Institutionalization of Commitment

When a commitment is made, it takes life in space and time, a given historical setting and era, within a framework provided by the free decision of the participants, community relationships, society and culture at large. Therefore, when we talk about a commitment to love God or another person, we have to deal with certain structures that we commit ourselves to as well. These are the concrete forms of living and acting that we commit ourselves to as an expression of love and as a means to love.

Many who have no difficulty experiencing themselves called to and responding in an unconditional commitment to God find that they have a lot of problems with the structures that the commitment is tied into. To be real, a commitment must be expressed in a context of interrelationships with family, Church and, for a Religious, a specific Religious community. One cannot expect to redefine or to reestablish the conditions of these relationships on a daily basis. Persons must live within a tradition, but at the same time avoid mindless submission to its customs and patterns.

Legitimate diversity within a given Christian community will ensure latitude for individual expression of commitment, for community support is essential to commitment. On-going commitment involves continuous re-election and re-selection, and all of those with whom and to whom we have committed ourselves figure in this process. That vital community support must be formalized or institutionalized in appropriate structures which, although ultimately arbitrary in themselves, ought not to be abandoned or altered without thoughtful and prayerful discernment.

Some Suggestions for Community Reflection on:

Commitment in a Changing World

After dialoguing on the thoughts below (taken from Sister Doris' paper), create a simple ritual in which all present can freely renew their commitment to God, and to significant persons and groups in their lives.

- Over-commitment at an earlier stage in one's life may bring on an "energy crisis" and consequent waning of commitment later.
- Although we may fear that passion will die in the process of commitment, we also fear the kind of death and waste of passion that comes from non-commitment.
- In an evolving relationship, the negatives of commitment — darkness, and dryness — have to be built into the life-process.
- Vital community support must be formalized or institutionalized in appropriate structures which, although arbitrary in themselves, ought not to be abandoned or altered without thoughtful and prayerful discernment.

8

Religious Life and Permanent Commitment: A Necessary Connection?

Kathleen L. Uhler, OSF

There is a necessary connection between Religious life[1] and permanent commitment. This means that without at least a core group of lifetime members, Religious life could not realize the full flowering of its two-fold objective of service to the people of God and of vocation as charismatic prophet in the Church.[2]

How is this so? First, the Religious community itself is a person, a corporate person, and from this it follows that whatever is necessary and good for the fulfillment of the individual person is required, for similar reasons, for the fulfillment of the corporate person.

A Religious Community is a Person

In which senses can we say that the Religious community is a person?

Sociologists tell us that as an individual person has stages of growth, so the corporate person, the organization, has an infancy, an adolescence — and hopefully, a maturity.[3] For example, Religious communities which are in the process of examining and renewing governmental structures are in the adolescent stage. Like the adolescent, the corporation is compelled to clarify its identifying structures.

The Religious community is a person because its governmental structure is collegial, that is, government by head and members. The collegial structure forms one body, a corporate person. Indeed, the Religious community, whether viewed as one local community or as an entire congregation, is an incarnation of the heart and mind of Jesus Christ.

Some psychologists and philosophers, such as Viktor Frankl and Gabriel Marcel, stress that full personhood requires dedication to a purpose or Thou that is greater than or transcends every temporal goal. Since the transcendent purpose or Thou outlasts all temporal goals, there is required implicitly a dedication which is life-long or permanent. The Religious congregation in adopting the evangelical and communal form of life embraces by the same act a transcendent or even eschatological form of life, an ideal to which the congregation aspires permanently.[4]

A Community as Corporate Person Requires Permanency for Its Future Fidelity

Now let us consider why Religious community as corporate person requires permanency to achieve its two-fold objective as servant and charism in the Church.

Basically, it is by force of the spiritual and corporal works of mercy that a Religious community is bound to expect and even to require a permanent commitment of its members. Without permanent commitment how could a Religious congregation plan realistically for the future regarding the ownership and care of corporate properties, its ability to promise service of significant quality and duration, the staffing and financing of various ongoing programs for its own members, such as Religious formation, professional preparation, and retirement?

Beyond meeting these and other requirements of life and service,[5] a Religious community must necessitate a permanent commitment from its members to guarantee the full flowering of its own commitment to the Church as charismatic prophet.

The Nature of Corporate Commitment

Let us consider the nature of this corporate commitment: the Religious congregation articulates in its constitution a commitment to the evangelical and communal form of life. The commitment is made to the Church and on its behalf. In principle, the commitment will not again be put in question. The will not to question the commitment again acts as a determinant of the future, of what in fact will be the case. But, ultimately for the Religious congregation, adherence to its way of life is held firmly only because of faith in its vocational grace. This means that the foundation of the vowed life and the "We believe" is the same: God himself. The stance of the corporate Religious person presupposes the realization of its own insufficiency and an unbounded hope in God's fidelity to bestow the vocational grace indefinitely.[6]

But clearly, the Religious congregation can pledge a commitment to God and the people of God, the Church, only to the extent that its members are required to pledge their commitment. Indeed, without the initial constitutional declaration that permanent commitment is required of its members, the Religious congregation has no sure basis for fidelity to its constitutional commitment to life and purpose which, for a perfect accomplishment, demands the strengths and gifts of adulthood: Middle-age with its charisms of self-sacrificing love and leadership; old-age, with its gifts of wisdom and the exemplification of the ultimate moment of Christian maturity, death in the Lord.

To sum up: For personal fulfillment, whether individual or corporate, a total commitment to a transcendent purpose or Thou is necessary; total commitment to a transcendent other implies life-long fidelity or commitment to it.

Implications For Membership and Formation Policies

We offer these further considerations:

If, then, permanency is necessary for the mature expression of Religious life, it follows that there should be a unanimity of minds and hearts regarding permanent commitment as a value. The constitutions and other official policy statements should be straightforward and consistent in articulating the necessity and justifications of permanent commitment as a requirement for membership.[7]

If permanent commitment is a necessity for the realization of Religious life, there should be an emphasis upon it in any introduction to the life.

Note well that following upon a corporate avowal of permanent commitment, a reasonable expectation would be the emergence of a core group or nucleus of life-long members. It is our contention, moreover, that in view of the total, life-long dedication implicit in the Religious commitment, it is also reasonable to expect the emergence and coherence of a core group which would consist of the vast majority of Sisters who make final commitment.

Permanence and Paradox in Dialogue

Several objections might be raised against the stated position that permanent commitment is necessarily connected with Religious life. We shall consider two such objections.

The logical conclusion of the argument is simply not upheld by the facts: statistics show that the "vast majority" of finally professed Sisters do not remain for life.

Our response is that what is argued here is not intended to reflect what is the case but what should be the case. We hold firmly to our conclusion in view of the psychological, sociological, and other evidences which indicate that personal fulfillment can be achieved only through total dedication to a transcendent other. In other words, permanent commitment in Religious life is a human good and, as such, it should "work."[8]

Admittedly, as Sister Margaret Mary Modde reveals in her report on departures from Religious life,[9] it is the impact of certain notions of the theory of person or personalism which has been a great influence in decisions to leave Religious life: one's consciousness is raised, and then the conclusion follows that in Religious life, "I am unable to be me!"[10]

Nevertheless, we all can be misguided: personalists variously claim that we are perfect just the way we are, that if we go deep within ourselves we can release there sources of creative and healing energies. From such reasonings it is easy to conclude, if not wise to do so, that ultimately one's destiny is a private affair.[11] Has such emphasis on self-will and self-actualization shaken credibility in the Religious way of life, the way to personal fulfillment through death to self?

Secondly, we Religious are simply part of our world in which permanence has died.

To the contrary. First of all, permanence has not died. Things that can change are changing faster, but the human ability to transcend temporalities forges relationships which are personally permanent and which become the vehicles for permanency in response: Wherever there is dialogue, there is truth; where there is love, many are made one; where there is community of hearts and minds, there is beauty. And conversely, a divorce, a break in a relationship, remains a human tragedy.

Furthermore, we maintain that Religious life is a part of the world but in the restricted sense of a counter-part, a paradox, in effect, where values are not ordered like those of the mainstream.

References

1.   The terms used here: "Religious life," "Religious community," "Religious congregation," apply only to institutes which require public profession of the evangelical counsels and community of life. Cf. "The Decree on the Appropriate Renewal of Religious Life" in *The Documents of Vatican II*, ed. Walter M. Abbott, SJ (New York: Guild Press, 1966), n. 26, p. 473.

2.   Cf. Ladislas M. Orsy, SJ, *Open to the Spirit* (Washington, DC: Corpus Books, 1968), "Prophets of the New Covenant," pp. 13-70.

3.   These stages of the growth of an organization overlap so that, while the characteristics of one of them predominates, traces of the other stages are also present.

4.   We believe that this adoption of a transcendent ideal of life decisively separates Religious communities from "total institutions." In Religious communities the transcendent ideal serves as a principle of organic growth, i.e., of community building; whereas it seems that in total institutions the lives of the members are managed according to the temporal principle or goal of containment *per se*. Cf. Sister Margaret Mary Modde, OSF, *Phase I: Research Project on Women Who Have Left Religious Communities* (Chicago: National Sisters Vocation Conference, 1975), pp. 3-5, for a treatment of Religious life *as* a total institution.

5.   We believe that these are all of the requirements which a "total institution" must meet.

6.   Cf. Gabriel Marcel, *Creative Fidelity* (New York: The Noonday Press, 1964), "Creative Fidelity," pp. 162-73.

7.   Other forms of on-going temporary membership are not precluded; however, we see a threat to the fulfillment of the transcendent nature and purpose of the Religious community should there be a preponderance of temporarily committed members.

8.   Cf. "Dogmatic Constitution on the Church" in *The Documents of Vatican II*, ibid., article 46, p. 77.

9.   Modde, *Project*, pp. 12-13.

10.   Cf. Richard W. Kropf, "Radical Commitment and Fulfillment," *Spiritual Life*, 21, pp. 75-92.

11.   Cf. Peter Marin, "Follies of the Human Potential Movement: The New Narcissism," *Harper's Magazine*, 251 (October 1975), 45-56.

Some Suggestions for Community Reflection on:

Religious Life and Permanent Commitment: A Necessary Connection?

- How do you think young Religious are responding to the image of a Religious community as a corporate person seeking a permanent commitment from its members so as to achieve its goal of being both servant and prophetic charism in the Church?
- Futurists do not underestimate the power of the self-fulfilling prophecy as an educative tool for moving into the future. Sister Kathleen implies that if a community articulates its belief in permanent commitment in its documents, that such a "will not to question" that commitment again will act as a determinant of the future, of fidelity. How can formation personnel best communicate to new members the reality that fidelity is both a gift and a process?
- If you agree with Sister Kathleen's conclusion that Religious life is meant to be counter-cultural in its witness to the value and possibility of permanent commitment, what do you see as meaningful in today's crisis and questioning of permanency?
- How do you envision membership in Religious communities in the year 2000 A.D.: small core groups of permanently committed members; vast majority of members permanently committed; other variations?

9

Women Religious, USA: Empirical Data on Vows

E. Nancy McAuley, RSCJ

A great deal of thought has been going into the revision of the Code of Canon Law. I would like to present a microcosm of some thinking of women Religious on the vows as stated in canon law. A recent study of Roman Catholic Sisters' understanding of their commitment through the vows generated significant implications for future formation.

Vows and Canon Law

The research I undertook was intended to investigate the extent of agreement and disagreement of women Religious (Sisters) in the United States with the vows of chastity, poverty, and obedience as spelled out in the canon law of the Roman Catholic Church. Although canon law was undergoing major revision during the research, the still-unchanged fundamental regulations concerning the Religious vows were established as the baseline for the study. Examination of relationships between pertinent background data and understanding of commitment through the vows constituted another aspect of the research.

The source of data was a case in point: a stratified random sample of five hundred Sisters of the International Coruniam Congregation (pseudonym used for Sisters under study), who were residing in the United States during the fall of 1973. Ten authoritative sources, consulted individually, selected the Coruniam

Sisters as most typical of women Religious in the United States today. The instrument constructed by the researcher was a mailed questionnaire based on canon law, subsequent Church documents, and current interpretative documents of the Coruniam Congregation. Seventy-five percent responded; the usable questionnaires totaled 373.

Data were analyzed in terms of percentage comparisons, since the instrument was designed to identify ambiguity and to search out target areas for future in-depth studies. Anonymous responses to the canon law definitions of the vows of chastity, poverty, and obedience were related to four demographic categories: number of years in Religious life, educational level, current occupation, and group living. Since the study was concerned primarily with basic commitment to Religious life, other data on the interpretation of the vows were analyzed summarily through composite tables showing general trends.

Slightly over half of the respondents perceived their commitment to Religious life in terms of the canon law definition. Substantial percentages fell into the "disagreement" categories, with a generalized ten percent being "undecided." Approximately three-fourths of the sample members agreed with the interpretative statement on the vows. Those in Religious life forty years or more tended toward agreement, with just the reverse true for those in Religious life ten years or less. Respondents in the highest and lowest levels of education tended toward agreement. The Master's level sub-sample consistently showed the highest percentage of undecided responses. Retired Sisters tended to agree, while student Sisters tended to disagree. Larger communities tended to agree, while smaller communities tended toward disagreement.

The substantial percentage of responses in the "undecided" and "disagree" categories indicates a discrepancy between what the Church officially states as commitment to Religious life and the way in which a substantial group of Roman Catholic women Religious perceive their commitment. The research raised many questions. Is there a lack of understanding of the canon law statements themselves? Have the statements become so far removed from the Sisters' daily living that they have become perceptually irrelevant? Is contemporary language so different from that of the

canon law statements that modern Sisters are unable to concep-
tualize in these older modes? Has the rising sense of individu-
alism taken so strong a hold on the mentality of Sisters that the
group culture of Religious life is no longer meaningful, or perceived in a different sense, or not perceived at all? Has female
self-awareness emphasized in the women's liberation movement
effected a tendency to reject group norms? A major question of
the times is: What should be the role of women Religious in contemporary life? Until the matter of commitment is worked
through, roles and behaviors cannot be properly determined.

Ambiguous Stance on Vows

The free write-in responses, not analyzed in this phase of the
study, underscored the ambiguous stance on the vows evident in
the structured responses. A cursory inspection of the free responses revealed significant data. Almost one-third of the entire
sample (32%) answered the open-end items, in addition to another third who wrote comments beside their structured responses. Fifty-seven percent of the respondents verbalized their
confusion about the meaning of the Religious vows today, even
though slightly over half of the entire sample checked the structured scale affirmatively.

A sizable group rejected the vows as defining their present
commitment. "All the 'legal' aspects really turn me off," wrote
one respondent, summarizing what many said, "because often
they lead to a great expenditure of time and energy in intellectual
arguments and theorizing, discussions, etc., which take away
from a true commitment to the simplicity of following Christ and
serving his people." Another in the 26-35 age bracket stated
openly what many of her contemporaries expressed in different
ways.

> My own commitment has very little if anything to do with vows. In
> fact, I don't think it ever did. The whole subject of vows passes me
> by completely. As long as Religious life remains wedded to the con-
> cept of these vows, it will never really attract creative, resourceful
> people. Perhaps the Spirit is calling Religious to another expression
> of their love. . . . The vows have proven to be distractions and obsta-
> cles to my becoming more Christian, human, and woman. My own
> commitment involves becoming whole in order to love others more
> fully.

About a fourth of the respondents looked upon the vows as a "medieval setup," and therefore historically relative: "Religious life can develop in other ways."

While a representative number of respondents from all age brackets chose to add write-in responses to their questionnaires, the 26-35-year-old sample members comprised 32% of the total number (N-119) who added write-in responses. Three young Religious who had completed their candidacy and profession formation within the past five years wrote the following remarks:

I feel that the answers or positions stated are most theoretical and ideal. The position and conditions of living the vows today are ambiguous — need re-evaluation and redefinition with newer insights of theology applied to them.

I see vows as giving a direction to my life so that I may grow into a more chaste, poor, obedient Religious committed to Christ. This to me is a dynamic understanding as opposed to the static idea of vows fixing one in a state. This in no way diminishes my belief that they are a definitive commitment.

I "agreed" with the more traditional interpretations of the vows because I could not "disagree," and I am not "undecided" about any aspect of them except whether the three are "of the essence" of Religious life, or whether one all-embracing vow would not do as well. As I see it, Religious life in our congregation today requires: 1) life in community; 2) celibacy; 3) simplicity of life; 4) prayer; 5) commitment to living gospel values. . . . In one sense, "poverty, chastity, and obedience" include these, but the focus is not as clear. I feel it is far more important than a Religious is committed to the five points I listed than that she is committed to the three vows as traditionally — or even currently — understood.

A 92-year-old respondent who has held many responsible offices wrote more copiously on her questionnaire than any other sample member.

I only disagree in spots. My own commitment is based on what was explained to me as a novice. It has held for 68 years — a constant spur and call to go steadily ahead in as completely a dedicated life as is possible to my limited understanding . . .

She is not averse to changes, but questions certain implementations, for example, "the bizarre costumes of some," referred to her as fitting Kipling's description of a woman: "a rag, a bone, and a hank of hair." Instead of checking the agreement-disagreement scale for the following statement in the congregation's renewal chapter documents, she asks for clarification. Regarding "The vow of chastity should give a new dimension to the sexual, emotive and creative powers," the 92-year-old respondent queries: "How can one know what this new dimension should be?"

A considerable percentage of the sample brought up the question of temporary versus permanent commitment. One answer captures the stance of the majority on this point. "I understand to some extent why some think permanent commitment unwise or impossible in this changing world, but I think this attitude reflects too much dependence on self or one's environment. . . . All really deep love seems to long for the 'forever' aspect in commitment as well as the risk implicit in such a commitment."

Approximately ten percent of the sample across the board voiced concern about initial formation programs, though not as strongly as one older individual: "I am appalled at the lack of real formation given lately to candidates aspiring to Religious life . . ." Most of the open-end responses were phrased in metaphorical terms. The question is: What do these metaphors mean to the respondents, and how do they translate them into specific behaviors?

Implications for Dynamism and Thrust Toward the Future

From the results of this basic study on the agreement and disagreement of Roman Catholic women Religious with the vows as stated in canon law, the researcher concluded that further examination of commitment in Religious life is imperative. The ambiguity, rejection, and openly expressed confusion regarding the vows call for inquiry into the type of Religious commitment that might be more appropriate to the mission of the Church today. Such matters as personal service, increasing comprehension of the world's peoples in all their diversities, the elimination of violent aggression against the human person, ecological balance in human existence, the enhancement of the intrinsic worth of every individual, require investigation relative to formation programs — both initial and on-going.

Vis-à-vis the Church's official regulation — that the three vows constitute one a Religious — it is important to determine whether a certain erosion of commitment is setting in among women Religious or whether new forms of Religious life are surfacing. It is equally urgent for Church leaders to hear the current thinking of women Religious of diversified ages and background, and to evaluate their lived (even if not vow-oriented) experience of commitment to Christ in the contemporary world.

Some Suggestions for Community Discussion of:

Women Religious, USA: Empirical Data on Vows

Sister Nancy's study, as well as the study done by Brother William Quinn (cf. *Sisters Today*, January 1972), indicates that there is a discrepancy between what the Church officially understands as commitment to Religious life and the way in which many American Religious perceive their commitment. *Discuss:*

- The fact that there is strong resistance to any suggestion of changing the traditional three vows in spite of evidence that these three vows as presently formulated do not dominate the lived experience of many Religious.
- The statement of the FSC Vow Committee that *undue* emphasis on the three canonical vows leads to an unhealthy standardization of Religious life and betrays the authenticity of each community. This committee suggests that it is the "special vows" that best express the unique character of each Religious family (cf. *The Brothers and Their Vows:* A Fresh Look at Religious Vows. Luke Salm, FSC, editor. Published by National Assembly of Religious Brothers, 1213 Clover Street, Philadelphia, PA   19107).

Reverend John Finnegan, past president of the Canon Law Society of America, in an article in the October 24 issue of the *National Catholic Reporter* (NCR, XII, 1, p. 2, 1975), refers to the post-Vatican II Church as going through stages of confusion, clarification, and finally integration. For him the Church is presently in the clarification stage, and has a need to live with ambiguity a little longer so that it will know what is characteristic of our Catholic life. He would like to see "repeated and successive changes in the law, a period of ad hoc-ism." Many others also favor a holding off on the revision of the new code in order to avoid a "fossilizing" of theological and pastoral developments in an immature state. At the 1975 annual meeting of the CLSA, some canonists advocated a continuation of ad hoc rulings and experimental guidelines.

- Do you think the Church will ever again be able to state the essence of Religious life in its canons? If so, when?
- How do you think the consultation on the new law should proceed?

The incorporation of new members into Religious communities can no longer be merely a process of assimilation. It must involve an on-going dialogue among all members with attention given to the dynamic character of Religious profession and the future-oriented nature of Religious life and the Church. Discuss the implications of:

- The fact that our full identity lies in the future and not in the past.
- The fact that human persons want to live in time and at the same time transcend it — that creative persons enjoy taking risks and shaping the future.

Three trends seem worthy of note:

- Current interest in futurism is leading people to place more emphasis on remaining open to future options and planning for change.
- Some young Religious who have the same distaste for notions of fixidity and permanence as many futurists are reluctant to make perpetual vows.
- Many seasoned Religious do not perceive fidelity as primarily a fidelity to structures, but as a person's fidelity to the inspirations and charisms which enable him/her to go forward in an on-going search for God and the living out of the gospel values.

If the above trends continue, what structures must be changed in order to nourish and forward the dynamism of today's youth, gifted with charisms and inspirations?

10

The Young Religious: Vowed To Whom? Committed to What?

Karen Gosser, SHCJ

When I first realized that my reflections on commitment would be shared in a dialogue on "Emerging Ministries," with the focus on formation for these ministries, I was a little unsure of how it would tie together. However, after reflection, I think that what I have to share as a young Religious is related in a very essential way to formation for emerging ministries.

Although our ministry as women Religious seems to be taking a variety of new forms, I think it is important to be conscious that they are all related to the mission of Jesus. Anyone focusing on the future must be aware of the kind of commitment Jesus called for and manifested in his own life.

I grow in my understanding of my commitment when I probe and contemplate the commitment of Jesus. The first part of my reflection centers on the gospel attitudes needed for the commitment that responds in service to the varied and complex needs of our global, interdependent society. Secondly, I will say something about what I think we are being called to in our commitment today.

Gospel Attitudes Necessary for Commitment

Jesus reminds us that no one can come to him who has not been drawn by his Father (John 6:44). Our vowed life ought to derive its energy and direction from a consciousness that we have been called, and drawn to union by God the Father's love. Edward Farrell puts it this way: "To be vowed is to enter into the mystery of Jesus saying, 'I am never alone, my Father is always with me . . . the Father and I are one.' "[1] To be one with Jesus in the Father means that we are called like him to participate in revealing the Father's love. Thus, we must be committed to doing just that.

To be one with Jesus in this way is to be ready to break with what is familiar and comfortable. "If anyone wants to be a follower of mine, he or she must renounce one's very self, take up one's cross and follow me" (Mark 8:34). Jesus calls for a commitment that demands that we turn from our own preoccupations and concerns and focus entirely on him. It seems Jesus is calling for the kind of emptiness or disposition that Paul refers to in Philippians, chapter 2, when he reminds us that our attitude must be the same as Christ's, who emptied himself, assuming the status of a slave, becoming so docile, so open and unassuming of his own greatness that he was totally open to respond to and reflect the desires of the Father's heart. As we reflect on commitment and the future, I would like to suggest that the cultivation of this emptying of self is an essential attitude for basic gospel or Religious commitment.

I see Jesus' commitment as foremost a commitment to the Father's will. In John's Gospel, Jesus tells his disciples that his food, his nourishment, is in doing the will of his Father (John 4:30). In Jesus' actions, we see what the Father was calling him to be and do. His life was a revelation of the Father's love for all men and women. This love was made real in the blind receiving sight, the deaf hearing, and mercy and justice being exercised on behalf of the needy and oppressed. As women vowed to live a life of union with God it would seem that we ought to be preoccupied with the Father's will and with the manifestation of that life in the world.

Attitudes Translated into Ministry for Justice

How are we to do this today? I believe that the Church's call to justice must be heeded and translated into action. The documents of Vatican II, recent encyclicals, and the statement from the 1971 Synod of Bishops make it clear that we are called to deal with the serious injustices present in our world and our responsibilities in relation to them.

Paul VI in his exhortation *On the Renewal of Religious Life Ac-*

cording to the Teachings of the Second Vatican Council asks
Religious: "How then will the cry of the poor find an echo in your
lives? That cry must, first of all, bar you from whatever would be
a compromise with any form of social injustice. It obliges you also
to awaken consciences to the drama of misery and to the demands
of social justice made by the Gospel and the Church."[2] The bishops, in their 1971 Synod Statement, call all committed Christians
to "action on behalf of justice and participation in the transformation of the world . . . as a constitutive dimension of the preaching
of the Gospel."[3] In this statement, they call us to broaden our horizons and our awareness of the needs of our world. These needs
call us, in our commitment, to grapple with our own position as
people who have power. This power is a consequence of our education, our having adequate food, shelter, income.

This call to awareness of the vast inequalities, subhuman living
conditions, and exploitation experienced by a good portion of the
world's peoples re-echoes the commitment Jesus calls for from
those who wish to participate in his kingdom. Jesus identifies
himself with the "least brethren" and makes it clear that what we
do to the least of our brothers or sisters we do to him.

Positive Imperatives

Father James Burtchaell in his book *Philemon's Problem* reflects
on this kingdom parable from Matthew's gospel, in which Jesus
points out that those who responded in love to the hungry, the
needy, the stranger did it to him and will be blessed with the life
of the kingdom. Burtchaell points out that those who failed to
address themselves to the miserable of the world may not have
violated any law and may very well have lived good lives. They
are guilty, he suggests, for what it never occurred to them to do.
The parable is disconcerting. God's claim was previously manage-
able and measurable. Our love of neighbor and commitment
today has no such easy boundaries.

Father Burtchaell suggests that the kind of activity we are
being called to today involves a positive imperative as opposed to
negative imperatives. Negative imperatives tend to be clear-cut.
We know when we have violated a negative imperative. For example, it is clear to us when we have been uncharitable. Likewise,
we know that perjury, embezzlement and adultery are wrong.

Most everyday life-decisions have to be influenced by this positive imperative. This means a consciousness of the needs of our times and the miseries of the world. The positive imperative motivates such decisions as what kind of work we do, what values we perpetuate, what political candidate we support, or what we buy or don't buy.[4] Perhaps this parable and the bishops' statement are calling us to expand our awareness and develop our ethical sensitivities to see the moral significance of our everyday life-decisions. Our commitment knows no boundaries in a world where almost all our actions have global ramifications.

Global Ministry Demands Nearness to Jesus

To love as he loved, to be women and men preoccupied with discerning the Father's will, is going to require a real sensitivity to the complexities of the injustice and suffering in our world. It will require a real freedom to move from the comfortable and familiar when we hear his cry to follow or respond to new challenges.

Bonhoeffer, in his book *The Cost of Discipleship*, points out that many of Jesus' followers found the demands of discipleship too great. He reminds us that the forces which tried to interpose themselves between the word of Jesus and the response of obedience are as formidable now as they were then. Reason and conscience, responsibility and piety all stood in the way . . . even the law and scriptural authority itself were obstacles to the whole-hearted commitment to the person of Jesus.[5] But integrally bound up in the challenges of commitment today is the invitation of the Lord, drawing us continually to deepen our lives of prayer and nearness to him. To remain committed to the kinds of challenges before us in a world marked by injustice and oppression requires that we remain very near to him. We must enlarge our vision of his grace and really believe that his power is at work in us in order to do infinitely more than we can ask or imagine.

Although I have not dealt specifically with any particular ministry, I think that a new consciousness needs to begin to pervade all our ministries. That consciousness must be a global consciousness. We must begin to ask ourselves: are we women that really hear the cry of the poor? How do we hear it? How does it echo in our lives? And further, how free are we? Do we possess that attitude that was Christ's? Have we emptied ourselves? I think that these questions are central to any reflection on formation for ministry in the Church today.

References

1.   Edward J. Farrell, *Disciples and Other Strangers* (Danville, N.J.: Dimension Books, 1974), p. 30.

2.   Pope Paul VI, *On the Renewal of the Religious Life According to the Teaching of the Second Vatican Council*, June 29, 1971, paragraph 18.

3.   1971 Synod of Bishops, *Justice in the World*, November 1971, Introduction.

4.   James Tunstead Burtchaell, CSC, *Philemon's Problem* (Chicago: Life of Christ, division of ACTA, 1973), p. 88-89.

5.   Dietrich Bonhoeffer, *The Cost of Discipleship* (New York: The Macmillan Co., 1966), p. 87.

Some suggestions for Community Reflection on:

The Young Religious: Vowed to Whom? Committed to What?

The first principle to guide Religious during this trying time of renewal and reform states that the gospel is to be the supreme norm and the judgment of our lives. Have we as community ever met to confront that statement of principle? Do we as a matter of fact accept the gospel as that norm and judgment of the way we live? The way we pray? The way we fulfill our ministry?

Reflecting on the commitment of Jesus to his own mission, what are the qualities of that commitment? Are these qualities present in us both individually and as a community?

The "emptying of self" is the phrase St. Paul used to summarize the commitment of Jesus to his divine mission. What are the implications in the life of our community? In what ways do we appreciate this value in the lives of the members of our community?

Jesus lived out his commitment in the midst of the people of his day. He was aware of their needs, their problems, their hopes, their struggles, their oppression. Our commitment requires the same awareness of us for our day. Do we as a community manifest this awareness? Do we seek to center our efforts in a true gospel love of Jesus and consequently of one another as we too reach out to the needy and the oppressed?

In a world where almost all our actions have global ramifications are we aware of the significance of and responsibility for our commitment as it affects the lives of others?

CARMELITE MONASTERY
LIBRARY
SARANAC LAKE, N.Y.

11

Why Women Religious Really Leave Communities

Margaret M. Modde, OSF

The NSVC-sponsored research on "Why Women Leave Religious Communities" will, I hope, provide material for serious study and prayerful reflection for all Religious, and especially for those in leadership and formation work. The study, co-authored with Dr. John Koval, should be read in its entirety before reflecting upon the questions below. My own reflection on this study has led me to a basic and, I think, important conclusion. It seems to me that a community has no right to receive new members into an initial formation program unless it also has an on-going formation program for all members. This question should be seriously considered by each and every Religious community.

The following reasons for leaving were cited most frequently by the women who left:

- community pressures;
- the lifestyle of the community;
- the lack of charity *within* the Religious community;
- the inability to be "themselves";
- the desire to marry;
- the desire for human intimacy.

It is hoped that after looking carefully at these reasons which the women who left gave, you will ask what the implications are for formation personnel and for members of communities. Perhaps only by further questioning and reflecting will we come to certain awarenesses. Such may be:

- How do we as Sisters sustain each other in our ministry?
- How can community pressures in this area and others be lessened?
- How can we bring about a rhythm in our lives that will allow for a balance of work, prayer, and leisure?
- Are we free enough to let our lives evolve — do we "hang on" to old structures through fear?
- Have we accepted many changes only on the intellectual level?
- How can we convey to women Religious the need for charity among themselves?
- Do we as women accept and respect the uniqueness of each individual in our Religious community?
- How do you deal with the question of intimacy in your life?
- How do you deal with the question of intimacy in the lives of others — in particular those persons who are in your community's formation program?
- How do you view the various levels of intimacy needed? Do you have an understanding of the degree to which a celibate community can meet these needs?
- What part does your total community have in your formation program?
- What concrete preparation do you give the community in order that they may better understand new members?
- What on-going educative programs do you have for your community members that approximate those of the initial formation program?

It is hoped that Phase II of *Why Women Leave Religious Communities*° will give you and your community material for serious study and prayerful reflection in the light of your own unique situation.

°For information on the NSVC study write to National Sisters Vocation Conference, 1307 South Wabash, Chicago, IL 60605: *Women Who Have Left Religious Communities in the United States*, A Study in Role Stress, Phase I, 1975; and *Women Who Have Left Religious Communities in the United States*, Phase II. Available 1976.

12

Initial Formation: Some Practical Considerations

Bernadette Marie Casey, RSM

As a formation director I am pulled in many directions by the overwhelming diversity of theory and opinion concerning formation to Religious life. Today there is ambiguity about "formation." Not only are the formation programs questioned, but the concept of formation is also being challenged. I have to face this dilemma daily simply because "formation" is my work: therefore, I wish to develop one thought which is reflective of my own experience.

I believe that the woman coming to Religious life does not know fully *why* she is coming nor does she know clearly *what* she is looking for. This is true notwithstanding her authentic desire to direct her life responsibly. I want to emphasize two aspects of this statement; namely, that a person may not know something about her own deepest experience; and, secondly, that because of this she has a need of formation.

Formation: Process and Program

What do I mean by formation? I mean simply the process and the program through which a woman becomes a Religious Sister, e.g., a Sister of Mercy. By perceiving formation in this way, I am trying to accent the necessity of both a program and a process through which a woman moves while personalizing the commonly held ideals of her particular Religious community. This ordinary (though profound) view of formation is, however, easily forgotten. There are likely many reasons for this, but I would like to isolate one reason which I believe has manifold consequences for the formation director, the initiate, and the future shape of our Religious communities.

Contemporary Religious life is characterized by diversity. There is no single model of contemporary Religious life to which all or even most members of a given community subscribe. But without at least an implicit model, the "end" (which shapes the entire process) becomes elusive, and it is not long before the entire process of formation becomes fragmented and diffuse. For example, if we specify the "end" of the formative process as the spiritual or psychological growth of the individual, the means we take to that end could be as simple as personal spiritual direction or psychological counselling. But if we envision the end of formation as "becoming a Sister of Mercy," the means to that end will of necessity be broader than either psychological counselling or spiritual direction. This is so because membership in Religious community already inserts one into a world of established and shared values, ideals and responsibilities. The formation process thus implies the communication and awakening of a whole way of living which we call the life of a Sister of Mercy.

Another way of stating the difficulty is to say that today we no longer have a "common way" for the process of formation. For instance in the past, we tried to communicate the spirit of our communities by encouraging specific practices that seemed to have shared history and acceptance among us, and which formed a common way. In formation we could say that this or that practice was part of our way. But today we have few common practices. Without wanting to encourage a return to an empty behaviorism or blind conformity, I nevertheless want to stress the fact that if formation is conceived, at least in part, as a process of communicating the spirit of our communities, and if the spirit is necessarily incarnate in everyday realities, then formation today is made especially difficult because "common ways" are no longer believed to be of special value.

Not Techniques but Atmospheres and Informed Disciples

To replace the common way and to reach for something to do in our formation programs, we are apt to jump from program to program and from cause to cause in search of the technique or activity that will individually or collectively form our ideal: a dedicated and responsible Religious woman. Our difficulty is that today, in searching for a way, we may neglect the rudiments for the development of such a woman: a stable community context in which to live, reliable and significant others, and the importance of ordinary means of deeper growth such as an informed discipline of sustained spiritual exercise.

What do these considerations mean relative to our formation today and what concern are they to us? Each of us must answer those questions in our own way and with respect for our own situations and understandings, but I would like to say two things about formation as we think about the future.

First, in formation work we must be primarily concerned with our fidelity to the original spirit and goals of our respective communities. Only then will we truly respond to the deepest needs of our candidates, that is, to be drawn *beyond* where they are into their own future.

Second, it is important to realize that we are responsible for our own future. Through our imagination, courage, patience, and work together, we will make the decisions that will shape our lives. In determining this future we are called to something more than an ability to adjust to our changing times, culture, and communities. We are called to something more than a natural resiliency in the face of life's difficulties and ambiguities. Our glory as persons is to dedicate all of our energies to shaping the direction of the life that we want to live in Christ.

Some Suggestions for Community Reflection on:

Initial Formation: Some Practical Considerations

The following areas of discussion might be more fruitfully explored by separating those in initial formation from those finally professed. After both groups have explored the questions, have them come together to reach a consensus on how initial formation is best carried out. If this is done at an intercommunity gathering, the new insights would be further enriched.

- Respond to Sister Bernadette's thesis that "a person may not know something about her own deepest experience" and that because of this she has need of formation.
- What have been some of the results of perceiving the formation of Religious as simply the growth of an individual through personal direction or psychological counselling?
- Sister Bernadette mentions three rudiments for formation in an age of diversity: a stable community context in which to live; reliable and significant others; the importance of ordinary means of deeper growth such as an informed discipline of sustained spiritual exercises. How can these elements be "programmed" in a creative and life-giving fashion?
- In determining the future, we are called to something more than an ability to adjust to our changing time, culture, and communities. What aspects of your community's formation programs (initial and on-going) are calling members beyond where they are and into a future where gospel values are cherished and lived?

13

Contemplation —
The Life Ministry Synthesis

Vilma Seelaus, OCD

There are many ways of approaching formation and its complexities. I will attempt to situate formation on its deepest level of reality. At this level, formation is not something new which begins when a person enters a Religious community; rather, it builds on a process integral to the person.

Our entire being comes into existence and grows as a response to the Word of God; and from a faith perspective, this is the basic human process which integrates all of life. The things we do are meant to be consonant with who we are, with our deepest self. For a life/action or a life/ministry synthesis to come about, we need to be attentive, to listen to the Word. God is always speaking to us: he is continually calling us forth. I believe that contemplative prayer is at the heart of the human process. This prayer is a looking toward, a listening to the Lord, the eternal Logos. Out of listening emerges the image or reflection of the self as mirrored in God's Word, and from this flows a sense of direction in life. The central focus of Religious formation, then, is to facilitate the process, to lead the person into a deeper relationship with God whereby the word God is speaking uniquely to the individual can be discerned.

I wish to develop the concept of contemplative prayer and life/ministry synthesis under the aspects of *person*, *process* and *program*.

Person in Dialogue with God

What is it to be a person? Philosophers and psychologists offer many helpful insights, but there is a deeper reality within ourselves which can only be grasped by faith in divine revelation, by reflecting on the mystery of our person as God reveals it to us. We come into existence in response to God's Word, created with a unique capacity for receiving and nurturing the Word in our heart. God's Word is to us a call, an invitation to divine intimacy. An incredible and loving tenderness is communicated.

In the creation story of Genesis, God adeptly forms clay in his image and carefully breathes into its nostrils the breath of life. Then he gently calls man and woman by name and they come to be. They respond to him as person to person. God is experienced as the partner of their humanity.

Herein is found the ultimate meaning of human existence: to be in dialogical relationship with God, our creator and father. We experience our relationship with him as a dynamic reality. Present in his Word, he continually calls us forth to greater fullness of being. It is *this* process which Religious formation is meant to foster. The mystery of Word and our response can be considered archetypal on the deepest level of human life and activity.

Process: The Experience of God

We are all very aware that responding to God is not an easy or automatic process. Our ancestors were unfaithful, and we too are unfaithful. Although we believe that God alone can call us forth, we experience our inability to surrender ourselves to him. To make this surrender in the dailiness of living requires a willingness to open ourselves to God in prayer, to take time with God. The Lord really wants to communicate with us, to reveal himself to us. The amazing thing is that in this experience of God, we come to an otherwise impossible quality of self-awareness. It is of such a quality that the awareness of God and the awareness of our deepest self become one awareness. At the inner core of our being, God reveals to us, through the movements and desires of our heart, the path our life is meant to follow. Out of the experience of God and of ourselves in him, a sense of direction in life takes shape.

How can we proclaim him whom we have not seen or heard? If

we have no personal experience of what it means to be saved from our sinfulness, from our anxieties, from helplessness, from alienation from our true self, then our efforts to communicate his message either by word or deed become futile. It is through the power of Jesus Christ that we are saved; it is Jesus who draws us to the Father. How can we be enthusiastic about the Father's love if it is not spoken out of a personal experience of this love? How can we be secure in ourselves in the midst of conflict if our security is not based on a surrender to his power at work in us?

The mystery of the Annunciation is the paradigm of personal surrender to the Word; for Mary had a listening heart. Were this not so, she could not have understood seemingly contradictory words — be virgin, yet mother. Though troubled and afraid, she was not overwhelmed. Mary responded, "How can this be done?"

The power of the most high would overshadow her. That which was to be born of her would be born of God. It was to be all his work, his gift to her. She had only to surrender herself to his gift to her. Mary was reassured, for the message was in harmony with her deepest self-awareness in God. She was of the *anawim* who received all from him, and so, simply, Mary said, "Let it be done to me according to your word."

Mary's surrender was not idle passivity. In the act of surrendering to God, Mary's whole being, body, psyche, spirit was totally caught up in the mystery taking place within her. Her sense of mission in life began unfolding.

In his concept of psycho-synthesis, Assagioli, the psychologist, writes of the need to discover the true self in order to harmonize life's choices. The recognition of one's real needs is an important aspect of discovery of the inner self as well as one indication of a person's life direction. It is only in looking at and listening to the Lord in prayer that we *fully* discover the way of truth being offered us. Our vocation and choice of ministry must be in harmony with the true self. The voice of community, of the Church, the needs of God's people, as well as our own authentic needs are all facets of the Word. Fidelity to this Word is something uniquely personal.

If we take our prayer life seriously, we will be able to resolve uncreative tensions and discover what the Lord wants of us as individuals and as community ministering in today's world. Otherwise our struggles to change unjust structures, relieve oppression, etc., leave us extremely vulnerable to becoming unjust and oppressive ourselves.

Program: House of Prayer as a Formative Experience

What has all this to say about formation? It has much to say, I think, about the quality of life of the Sisters directing formation. A contemplative attitude, receptivity to the Word, cannot be taught. These are communicated through persons of significance in the lives of those in initial formation. The example of integrated, praying women is much more convincing than lectures on the value of prayer, helpful as these are.

With contemplative prayer as the heart of formation, spiritual direction or competent guidance in prayer is essential. It enables the novice to cultivate a listening heart, to discern the illusions of the false self, to recognize the unique gift that she is, and to share her gift confidently as the Lord leads her. Opportunity for competent counselling seems an accepted norm in formation today; hopefully, spiritual direction will be given equal importance in the future.

The Church's recent insistent teaching on social justice has prompted many communities to provide novices with an experience of ministry during the early years of formation. This seems to awaken a deep desire to be involved in the liberation of people. I would like to suggest something which at first seems unconnected with social justice, but which I believe is quite related.

Last December, I had the privilege of participating in the Monroe Conference II, the five-year evaluation meeting of the House of Prayer Movement in the United States. It was a rewarding experience. As a result of the experience, an idea has come to me which I offer for your consideration. Apostolic experiences have been of value to formation. Does not the House of Prayer also have something to offer? Recently, a young Sister who expressed the desire to spend time in a House of Prayer was discouraged from doing so, for this was considered an escape from the pressing needs of today's apostolate. The feeling was that in apostolic community she should be moving in the direction of involvement. Without responding to these objections, I would like to share a few thoughts in support of a House of Prayer experience for new members.

Spiritual values offered during the first years of formation may not touch the novice at that time, for God has his own moment. As the faith-life significantly awakens, however, it could give birth to a genuine desire for greater solitude and silence. Without creating a "hot-house" environment in the novitiate, a House of Prayer experience could well provide an atmosphere for the Word to implant itself more deeply in the novice's heart. From this desert experience apostles could emerge more attuned to the Lord and more genuinely sensitive to the needs of his people, women better able to cope with the ingratitude, failure, and other difficulties of ministry. A person who has experienced the Lord draws others to him by her very being. Her life has repercussions far beyond the immediate sphere of her activity.

This became clear to me early during one of my morning walks along the beach near our monastery. The bay was unusually calm, but I heard a sudden strong swish of incoming surf. I assumed it was the changing of the tides, until I turned and scanned the waters. In the far distance, a small one-man fishing vessel was speeding its way across the water. As the small craft disappeared in the direction of the islands, the waters again became calm and unruffled. I have experienced this phenomenon many times since, but it never ceases to amaze me how these small boats can affect such large expanses of water and change the face of the distant shores. The same is true of us. The words of Paul come to mind: "His power working in us can do infinitely more than we can hope for or imagine."

Houses of Prayer differ in their orientation, so there would be need for careful selection. It is important where a person goes, and that she keep in touch with the formation personnel and particularly with the movements and events in her community. Spiritual direction would be essential during this period. The span of this time should be long enough to allow the person to discover her own inner rhythm of prayer.

The needs of the apostolate will always be greater than our ability to fill them; but if a novice surrenders to God's Word taking root in her heart, the fruit of her life will transcend the immediate sphere of her activity. Her sense of identity will not be exclusively in the things she does, but in the awareness of herself as precious to the Father. Her response to the needs of people will not be out of ambition or out of guilt, but as a sharing of the Father's love. In the difficult moments of the future when the enticement of an exclusive love or the opportunity for an attractive career open before her, the Religious woman formed and nourished by the Word will, like Mary, question the Lord to see how these things resonate with her deepest self-awareness before Him.

Some Suggestions for Community Reflection on:

Contemplation — The Life Ministry Synthesis

Read and reflect on the word from scripture. After sharing prayer, ask the group to reflect first in small groups, and then as a total group, on the following:

- Sister Vilma presents contemplative prayer as the heart of the formation process. She describes this prayer as a looking toward, a listening to the Word. Out of such looking and listening emerges the image or reflection of the self as mirrored in God's Word and from this flows a sense of direction in life. If the central focus of Religious formation is to facilitate such a delicate process, what are the qualities you would look for in a novice director?
- Sister Vilma sees "being in dialogical relationship with God in the mystery of Word and our response to it as an archetype of the deepest level of human life and activity." What experiences have been most helpful to you in your efforts to enter more deeply into this mystery of faith?
- It is for us, as for Mary, only in listening to and looking at the Lord, in prayer, that we fully discover who we are and what our mission is. How can this insight be related to the current need and search for ways to discern choice of ministry, local community living situations, second-careers, retirement ministries?
- Sister Vilma suggests that a House of Prayer experience might help prepare a novice for the future because it provides an atmosphere for the Word to implant himself more deeply in the heart. She further suggests that the novice would come from such an experience more sensitive to the needs of people and better able to cope with the difficulties of ministry and life. Would such a formative experience be encouraged in your community for Sisters at any stage of formation — novices, middle-aged, retired Sisters? What other untried formative experiences would you like to introduce into your formation program?

14

Today Decides Tomorrow: Vocation in a Changing World

Ann Heilman, SFCC

I have two images of Religious life. One is of traveling in fog or darkness, able to discern far off against the sky the goal toward which I move, but unable to make out more than a step or two of the way that lies ahead. I know where I am going and with whom, but not how to get there. This isn't troubling, for the *how* takes care of itself if I go forward as far as I can see my way. From the new place I'll be able to see farther. The second image is of swinging through space from one suspended ring to another. To do this you must let go the first ring before you grasp the third. If you are afraid to let go, you can't move forward.

These images reflect an experience of Religious life that is deeply rooted in the past and wide open to the future. The commitment to go forward in faith and love wherever it leads is at the heart of the process of Religious life. Around it the whole person of the Religious is formed and integrated and on it depend her continuing fidelity and personal growth. Daily, this commitment is her touchstone for decision-making and the force that lures her forward into a fuller and more radical response.

Religous life is presently undergoing a painful but healthy and necessary process of shaking loose from old anchor points so that a new integration and conformation can take place which will fit it to meet the changed needs of the era we have already entered. New forms will arise, and older ones will be lived in new ways because those living them will come from cultures with different needs, experience, expectations and competencies. We now seem to be in the midst of one of the four or five great transition periods in Religious life. In the past, major transitions took place when monasticism arose as an alternative to the desert life; when the mendicant preaching orders presented a radical alternative to monasticism; and when new orders and congregations dedicated to the active service of Church and humanity inaugurated an era of concentration on works.

New Lifestyle in Response to Current Needs

Toward what are we in transition? For clues to the answer let us look first for needs in society which seem to be widespread but essentially unmet, and second, for phenomena which point a direction.

Historically, Religious life has always changed in ways that reflect societal and personal needs. How can we know which social changes today have produced the needs to which Religious life must respond with imagination and compassion if it is to know a fresh upsurge of life and vitality? At close range an adequate perspective is not possible, but one may discern a few important elements of the design.

The first is the fact that frequent, rapid change has come to characterize life. Here three things will be demanded of those who will be successful in mastering and transcending our environment-in-flux; 1) the stability of an inner core of relatively explicit, self-consistent and internalized values; 2) an inner openness to experience; and 3) the habit of frequently evaluating and reviewing goals and strategies.

Related to the factor of change is the experience of rootlessness and lack of meaningful connectedness with persons and institutions, which today seems to be endemic. This condition strikes at very basic needs to belong, to feel safe, and to be valued. To respond to it there is need for risk-taking personal involvement in the lives of people who are alone and afraid.

A third significant change is in the amount, quality, and kind of knowledge current in our society. The proportion of people who are well educated and informed is greater today that it ever has been. Some of our knowledge comes, via communications media, with an immediacy and directness of experience which produces self-involvement and facilitates responsive action. Educated people are increasingly aware of the fact that the choices made in their generation may very well be fateful for future life on earth, and with that knowledge comes responsibility.

Once we see ourselves in relation to a need, an injustice, the averting of a danger, our obligation to act must at least be honestly and generously weighed. We have entered an age of increased and increasing personal responsibility, and this kind of responsibility cannot be discharged at an institutional level. Organizations are responsive and innovative only as individuals influence them. There is no sheltering from individual responsibility, for not to know is not an excuse when we have the tools of knowledge at hand. Corporate inertia is not an excuse; if everyone has overslept, the first one awake must call the others.

SFCC Phenomenon Points a Direction for the Future

A phenomenon of present-day Religious life which points a direction for the future is the existence and very growth of Sisters For Christian Community. It is now five and one-half years since Lillanna Kopp publicly announced "a non-canonical nucleation of contemporary Christian women gathering together from traditional congregations and orders who wish to continue our commitment to Christ within currently-to-be-explored religious lifestyles." Since then over four hundred and fifty women have become members of SFCC. Of these, twenty have been able to resolve matters and return to their communities, while about a quarter of the young women who had no prior experience of Religious life (about three percent of the total membership) have come to feel the need for more direction and entered traditional congregations. Fifty women have left for marriage or for unspecified reasons. Three have died. The membership in 1975 stood at about 375.

No community would grow unless it were meeting important needs. The first need is for a vehicle through which Religious women who voluntarily or involuntarily have left their congregations can live out their vocation in a full and open way. Their lives have been built around the centrality of their vocation; these women have no desire to give up their vocation when they feel themselves called to live it in a new form, when they are eased out, or when for their own survival they feel that they must leave. Luigi Rulla, SJ, has written that Religious vocation establishes and forms the very existence of the person and binds together the private and public areas of human existence. For me, the experience of coming into SFCC was a liberating one. It met my deep need to be outwardly what I was interiorly, to be all-of-a-piece. My private shorthand for what it meant after years on my own was "going public." We can expect this kind of need to continue, although hopefully at a diminishing rate, until the transition has been effected to the next era of Religious life.

We have seen that some kind of alternative form of Religious life is presently needed. What then are the characteristics of Sisters For Christian Community which suggest directions in which Religious may see themselves moving in the near future? It is helpful, in understanding SFCC's rapid growth, to take a look at the SFCC Profile, Lillanna's description of the projected community. The apostolate is spelled out: "Our primary apostolic goal is to witness the uniqueness of Christian community. We agree with Vatican II's statement that the era of concentration on works is ending, and that of *penetration* is before us. In this opening era each Sister will determine her own penetration role on the basis of her time, training and temperament. She will be yeast for Christian community in whatever work or living structure she penetrates. Yeast must be within dough, not alongside it. We seek to elevate the value system of the total society."

Structure: "We recognize from the gospel that Jesus gathered together a community of believers whose specifying character would be mutual love and helpfulness. During the course of decades the Church moved slowly into a bureaucratic mode of organization, thereby confounding and alienating some members. Our goal, as stated simply in our title, is to help return the Church on every level to the community principle of organization and service. We will avoid becoming a formal organization. By design, we are simply a free-form unity of persons gathering together in community in Christ. We are united not by rule and constitution but by mutual concern and communication. . . . We will be collegial in any decision which affects the community."

The goal: "We strive through all means available to forward the realization of Christ's prayer: 'that they all may be one' . . . that they may be community."

The form of expressing commitment: "The traditional vows will give way to a simple statement or promise to give witness to Christian community in a celibate state. Each Sister is self-employed and self-supporting. Poverty in this contemporary free-form community is not concerned with the quantity of money held but with the Christ-like relationship and services it facilitates. Poverty in this context becomes loving availability. Obedience follows St. Thomas Aquinas' simple definition: the conformity of the will to right reason as directed toward the common good."

The freedom of Sisters to arrange how and where they shall live: "Some may need or prefer to live alone at times, but even then community will be effected through on-going communication. Sisters know from experience that physical togetherness and geographical proximity do not by themselves create community. Community transcends distance. It is the warmth and security one experiences from shared love-in-Christ, shared confidence, shared concern, shared risks for Christ."

This is the promise that drew the first members and that still draws many inquiries. Beyond this is the reality of valuing our diversity and one another's uniqueness. Every stream of spirituality and both the active and the contemplative life are represented among us. We discuss formation in terms of *becoming,* so that instead of being divided on the question "formation for what?" we can unite in helping one another become all that God wants us to be. There is the reality of an unquestioning welcome and of warm affirmation. Above all, there is the modeling that we do for one another of how this new kind of Religious woman can live her life and fulfill her mission of being leaven wherever she may be: of loving with Christ's love and drawing others together in love.

Implications for Formation

Both the new needs of the world, and the SFCC lifestyle indicate that Religious life in the future will have to produce persons who know what they are about and why, who have worked to internalize their own self-consistent value systems, and who are mature and centered enough to be able to respond to others in a fully human way — no longer can response be merely in terms of their roles, professional or Religious. This is necessary if Christ's love is to be made *effectively* present in the world today and tomorrow. Although Religious life has produced a splendid flowering of mature, responsible, caring women in every age, including the present, it hasn't produced them in the proportion we have the right to expect and strive for, nor has it always been comfortable with those it has produced.

If Religious are to respond effectively to present and future needs, those charged with formation responsibilities must be given the best preparation available. This should include the opportunity to attain sufficient self-knowledge and objectivity to be aware of at least some of the ways in which they may tend to let their own feelings and expectations influence their perceptions and decisions. What is most important is that they themselves be searching, responsible women, growing in love and maturity in Christ and in him free to love and to share themselves. Next in importance is that they model values and principles they wish to teach.

It is a huge job educators have in helping people become capable of solving moral questions on a principled level and of internalizing the values they consciously hold. Research indicates that only twenty percent of the adult population of this country solves artificially posed dilemmas of moral conflict at the level of principled thought. Of these a substantial number (in one small sample, twenty-five percent) do not act in a way consonant with their principles. Other research suggests that when basic human needs for love and esteem have not been adequately met, this constitutes a hindrance to attaining the middle and higher levels of moral reasoning. The person, locked in on self, cannot as readily see situations in other than immediate, personal terms. Other investigations point to a relationship between low esteem and perceiving one's self as unable to participate in the process of meaningful decision-making.

Supportive Communities for Ministry

The ministry of leaven and the task of building community in the world can take us anywhere. There will be confused, alienated people who don't see meaning or hope in their lives in every stratum of society, among the middle-class as surely as among the poor, and we must be there for each of them individually. Only by risking a real commitment to knowing and being known, to loving and being humanly and untidily loved back, can we carry Christ's entirely gratuitous love to persons to whom the institutional Church is irrelevant or to those for whom the idea of a disinterested love is unthinkable. Sisters feeling themselves called to this most healing of ministries will need to know themselves well and have a more than academic knowledge of human psychology. This will also need the support of a community which correctly understands the legitimacy and value of their ambiguous role and encourages them to be where they are needed.

We are all in need of continuing formation, of helping one another in the becoming process, for the future will be concerned with what we are, and do as persons. I don't know what will happen in regard to SFCC. Conceivably, if its goals are accomplished and become part of the fabric of Religious life as that comes to be lived in the future, we could phase ourselves out of existence, because there is no need for any group to perpetuate itself once the reasons that have called it into existence have passed. On the other hand, change goes on at such an accelerating rate that pioneering is in no danger of going out of style. The future is open.

If we go forward in faith as far as we can see; if we let go of the good we hold in order to grasp the good we are approaching, then: "Think not you can direct the course of Love, for Love, if it finds you worthy, directs your course." — Kahlil Gibran

Some Suggestions for Community Reflection on:

Today Decides Tomorrow: Vocation in a Changing World

We know that new visions and new forms both threaten and encourage. We also know that organizations are only as responsive and innovative as the persons who influence them, and that "if everyone has overslept, the first awake must call the others." It is evident to most Religious that the

Sisters for Christian Community have and continue to meet important needs in the lives of many Sisters.

- After reflecting upon the excerpts from the SFCC Profile, point out ways you think that SFCC has and will continue to influence the future of the Religious life in the United States.

By design, SFCC is simply a freeform unity of persons gathered together in community in Christ. The Sisters are united not by rule and constitutions but by mutual concern and communication. They intend to avoid becoming a formal organization.

- After reflecting on both the potential and problematics of such a loosely structured community, share what you think other communities might learn from SFCC's attitude toward formation as described in Sister Ann's paper.

In speaking of trends, Sister Ann mentioned three qualities that will be demanded of those who will successfully master and transcend an "environment-in-flux": the stability of an inner core of relatively explicit, self-consistent, and internalized values; an inner openness to experience; the habit of evaluating and revising goals and structures.

- From your experience, share what formative atmospheres and experiences best bring about and/or deepen such qualities in Religious.

Sister Ann mentioned as a trend the lack of meaningful connectedness with persons and institutions, which today seems to be endemic. She suggests that this condition in our society strikes at the very basic needs to belong, to feel safe, and to be valued.

- How do you feel this trend has influenced the following: the great number of Sisters who have left Religious life; the Sisters who have transferred from one community to another; Sisters breaking from a community to form a new community; the Sisters who have "psychologically" left their communities.

15

Formation of Transferred Sisters: Some Realizations and Hopes

Maria Gatza, IHM

Is continuing formation a value that seriously enters into the conscious attention of either "transferred" Sister or the "new" community, once transfer has occurred? This question rises rather naturally in my mind as my ministry periodically brings me into contact with Sisters who are either hoping to transfer or have already done so. In this ministry, I am concerned with the well-being of persons, as *persons*.

That a community maintain a positive thrust toward the ongoing growth of its members, whether or not transferred, seems highly desirable. If a community can develop a style of continuing formation in which its members are affirmed, in which their personal goals are enhanced, and helped to contribute to the corporate goal, its ministry to the Church and to the world is thereby greatly strengthened.

Individualized, Non-Stylized, and Dynamic Programs

Essential to developing this style of life is the concept that the entire span of human life, together with each of its processes, revolves about certain rhythmic changes: building up, tearing down, renewing, and forging ahead.

In this thought pattern, persons are of supreme value. Because each of us constantly experiences the dynamism of rhythmic change, what we "do" to another person must be done with great sensitivity. Consequently programs, plans, systems, may benefit; or they may prove detrimental. Only to the extent that it supports the basic affirmation of the worth of a person is any plan used to achieve dreams and goals worthwhile.

If a plan or process used to "induct" Sisters who have transferred is to be considered properly formative, it seems to me that it must provide for the enhancement of the personal gifts of the individual while, simultaneously, furthering the community thrust. I decided to consult some Sisters who had already transferred. Others, perhaps, could benefit from their sharing.

My research involved a small number of Sisters, limited to those who had transferred within the past ten years to the Monroe Branch of the Sisters, Servants of the Immaculate Heart of Mary. It was conducted informally through the Sisters' written responses to a letter from me, through phone conversations and personal visits. The questions I asked them were simply put:

> What *formative factors* contributed toward your ease of entry into the new congregation?
>
> In what respects would you have liked the situation to have been other?

Rather than term my "results" as conclusive in any way, I choose to present them as hopefully thought-provoking comments which may be helpful to others.

Among the responses of the Sisters participating, three strong preferences seemed to enjoy almost universal support.

- Any "formation programs" considered should be individualized to fit the needs and circumstances of the Sisters in question;
- transfer-Sisters should be encouraged to profit from the ongoing formation opportunities open to all other Sisters within the congregation; as part of continuing formation for all, transfer should be seen more generally as a positive and good way for a Religious to continue faithful to that call which was given to the individual by the Spirit.

Each of these thoughts, in turn, deserves some fuller development.

Individualized Programs

According to the Sisters surveyed, both the transfer-Sister and the new community stand to profit from an individualized approach at the time of initiating relationship. For one thing, each can thus take the time needed to come to appreciate the gifts and talents of the other, while learning, in less pressurized circumstances than otherwise, how to look at any possible limitations on either side as less threatening. Compressing either a human person or the community itself into a static program, no matter how simple such a plan may appear when laid out on paper, can not match results with letting the Spirit run free in both the Sister and the community.

It may be less tidy to proceed in this fashion and may even take more communicating and negotiating but, in the long run, both the Sister and the community will profit. Let's look at a few comments drawn from my sample which highlight some thoughts on this topic.

"I would have chafed at being put into a special formation program imposing a structured manner of *being* and *doing*," explained one Sister. "I believed that I was, at that moment in my life, already a formed Religious and no more wanted to start over, as it were, than to remain at that point where I was. I thank the Lord that my transfer occurred the way it did, even though a few of the basic steps were painful."

A second Sister indicated that had she felt pressured toward "patterning" while she was becoming acquainted with her new community, a certain freedom of reflection which she needed in order to arrive at her moment of decision would have been lacking.

For yet another transferee, freedom to individualize her approach made it possible for her first to opt for a more casual, informal mode of learning about the new community. Later, when she experienced "impatience with herself" because her "settling in" was not "happening faster," she was able to change plans. This Sister found her greatest growth occurring only after she moved into the novitiate house, undertook an ambitious self-initiated study program which involved several months of research into IHM community history and charism, and experienced broadly based personal interviews with various community members, and a semester's exposure to theology course work.

At this point, perhaps a word of explanation would be suitable, lest I convey the impression that Sisters asking for individualized

approaches toward entry into the new community displayed negative attitudes toward formation itself. To do so would be untrue
to them, and to the facts of reality.

Each Sister, under the direction of her authority-person, was
provided community work, community residence, and a plan
whereby not only would she familiarize herself with the congregation during her year of "living-in," but also the congregational
members (its officials, and to whatever degree possible, wider
membership) would come to know the Sister to such an extent
that decision-time would not find either unknowing of the other,
at least in essentials.

The focus for emphasis in this, therefore, is centered on the ad-
vantages accruing from non-stylized, dynamic, and individualized programs, not on whether there should be any program at
all.

Availability and Adaptability of Continuing Formation

A second, strong preference expressed by the Sisters whose opinions I surveyed was that transfer-Sisters be encouraged to profit
from the on-going formation opportunities open to all other Sisters
within the congregation. Each one, in turn, favored wide-spread
positive community support of "continued formation" in terms of
"dynamic growing experiences," "continuing religious growth,"
"maturing life experiences," "deepening one's experiences of Religious life," and the like. "On-going formation," one Sister assert-
ed, "not in terms of programs, but in terms of personal growth
which can be fostered in multiple and individual ways is for *all*
Religious — for all persons — whether one remains in her first
congregation or changes to another."

The Sisters were quick to observe that on-going formation opportunities, whether informal or more formalized in nature, are
actually more abundant than we realize. In fact, in our daily rush
to "get things done," we undoubtedly let many of them pass by.
A couple of examples of how even an atmosphere favorable to
growth can be formative might crystallize this concept:

"I experienced very shortly after arriving," one Sister confided,
"a settling effect of belonging, of being at home. I attributed that
sensation to an atmosphere of love and acceptance of me which I
found in my new community. As time went on, I became more

conscious, too, of an enhancement of my *own* sense of personal security resulting from frequently experiencing the warm concern which I saw one Sister show for another."

"I no longer think a lot about belonging to my former community," another Sister quietly ventured, "except to be grateful to the Lord for calling me, and for continuing to call me to fidelity to himself. The greatest growth factor of my life involved my discovering a need to operate out of love, to be totally open to letting failure happen without fearing it. But I suspect," she added after a moment's reflection, "that that would have been good for me even had transfer not been part of the history of my religious commitment."

Informal, or more casual formation, then, happens moment-by-moment. "I'd say my thoughts and outlook are constantly being refined," one Sister concluded, "by exposure to a variety of opinions, attitudes, and convictions of Sisters of all ages. I relish the chance to learn community history and customs from its living members."

In addition to informal formation, more formalized opportunities in the form of workshops, lectures, and weekends are often available, and these are, in the words of one transfer-Sister, "great occasions for examining, weighing, challenging and accepting."

Just for the sake of verifying, I checked back on the community offerings of even the last two-year period and discovered a rich number and variety of opportunities which had been made available, each one in some way capable of furthering the formation of participants. There were workshops on leadership for local communities, on the elimination of self-defeating behavior, on communications; a day on explaining the theme of "Women for Woman"; opportunities to pursue the meaning of "Christian Ministry Today and Toward Tomorrow"; Days of Prayer, liturgical experiences, sharings in community prayer, "Hermit Days," Penance Services, and times to be individually directed through long or short retreats. Other workshop topics called us toward the development of an apostolic spirituality; toward greater fidelity to discernment in our lives; toward fuller understanding, and more recently, to bicentennial activities.

Some of these opportunities brought only members of the community together; others involved Sisters with lay people, and with Religious of other communities, priests, and Brothers — so that richness of result could flow not only from the topic under consideration, but also from contact with other mature adults.

With opportunities for pursuing one's continued Religious and personal growth so amply in evidence, it seems doubtful that the desire of transfer-Sisters for on-going experiences would be lacking. Further, with varied offerings, it is possible for growing and learning to take place in concert with other members of the community, a feature from which Sisters coming new to community appear to derive a sense of enjoyment and great benefit.

Transfer: A Valid Way to Remain True to Call

A third and final preference expressed by the women I contacted was a strong plea that transfer from one community to another be more generally regarded by those in and out of Religious community as a positive and good way for a Religious to continue faithful to that same initial call which was given her by the Spirit. Consequently, I found that transfer-Sisters did not respond favorably to a suggestion made in an earlier article of mine (cf. *Review for Religious*, May, 1975, pp. 358-365) that "sinking permanent roots . . . twice in the space of a human lifetime" might not be possible. For these Sisters, transfer is not only possible — it has touched their lives and become a reality. For them, it is a viable way to go when it is no longer within their original community that they can hear the call of the Lord. Consider some of their testimonials:

"I look at my transfer as an unbroken continuation of what was begun. One cannot limit the Spirit." [Reminiscent of that selection from Bernstein's Mass: "You cannot imprison . . . scuttle . . abolish the word of the Lord."]

"Transfer, for me, was a juridical procedure which set a new rhythm of life into being."

"I am convinced that my basic vocation never changed — just its mode of expression which had been stifled, in certain respects, in the mother-community."

"A new home-base gave me greater freedom to live the redemptive mission of Christ in the footsteps and with the attitude of Mary, in greater fullness and richness."

"My personal 'gut' feeling was not one of transferring, but of living the same vocation in a richer, deeper way — in another home."

While each Sister testifies to her experience of continuity of call throughout the transfer process, some express more clearly than others why they think this was possible for them.

"The Sisters, in showing a warm concern for me," stated one, "consistently made attempts to integrate me as a member of their community. They made me feel they trusted that I would help to incarnate the same values which they prized, so that together we grew as a faith community."

While they recognize the differences between one community and another (resulting from varying charisms of different founders), they very much hope that the essentials of Religious vocation will be seen as commonly shared by all Religious communities. And they, like us all, try to deal healthily with fears which arise. If any fears are more typically those which transfer-Sisters may have to meet squarely, they are those which center on spending years being thought of as a "group apart," or as "unstable," or "outsiders," and therefore incapable of giving constructive input to the community.

They fear having no identity except in terms of having transferred: "This is M; she used to be a such-and-so Sister." Or, in apostolic work situations, they dislike being introduced as "Sister who *was* . . ." when it would be more appropriate to be introduced positively in terms of job competence and performance, as would be any other member of the community, given the same circumstances. When pursued with the questions, "What do they do in *your* community?" five years after transfer into the elected community has been finalized, a Sister experiences an inner ache in replying, "I'm one of *you*," and wonders how much longer she must live among them before being taken "for real" in the minds of some members.

If there are any hopes that transfer-Sisters would voice, they center on having these fears diminished, to the end that they may give themselves fullheartedly, with the rest of us, to the mission of service to the poor and needy of the world, as members of the Church, and of the community. They have come — through many sorrows, at times — to view transfer for themselves as a mature and courageous act capable of freeing further personal powers because of the Word they have heard spoken deep within their beings. They will be glad when many others are able to envision transfer that way too.

I began this paper wondering whether continuing formation is a value which activates the conscious attention of either "transferred" Sister or "new" community, once transfer has taken place. I am satisfied now that, while there will always be a need for better implementation, the values *are* present and, hopefully, future-oriented. Human history has a direction; and no segment of that history is ultimately without meaning. That meaning is, when all is said and done, life-giving.

Some Suggestions for Community Reflection on:

Formation of Transferred Sisters: Some Realizations and Hopes

- Most Religious experience fidelity in Religious life as both a gift and a process. Share your feelings about the expressed hope of transfer-Sisters that "as a part of continuing formation for all, transfer may be seen more generally as a positive and good way for a Religious to continue faithful to that call which was given her by the Spirit."
- In your experience, what have been the hopes and fears of communities who have had Sisters transfer from them to another community. Are they the same, or different, for communities who have received Sisters who are transferring into their community?
- What do you foresee for communities who are open to new forms of membership?
- How do you envision formation in a community with several styles of membership?

A Dialogue on Emerging Ministries

The papers in this section attest to the fact that ministry, spirituality, and lifestyle all shape one another. The implications of this for formation personnel and community planners are many. Sister Vincentia Joseph's paper is concerned with the preparation of Sisters for their first, for new, and for second-career ministries. She stresses the need for new attitudes and structures in Religious life and for new ways of preparing Sisters for ministry. Sister Ann Gormly wonders if formation personnel are asking the right questions about mission, Church, and vows. She holds that an older and narrower view of Church and mission will not support newer styles of community life and service. Sister Margaret Ebbing gives personal witness to the expansion of mind and heart that can come to anyone willing to push out from the walls of traditional forms of ministry to become involved in "third world" ministries.

Sister Shawn Copeland and Sister Maria Iglesia, spokeswomen for Black and Hispanic Sisters, tell of the need to recognize and value the presence and contributions of Sisters from various races and cultures. They call attention to the need to recognize and celebrate these differences in our formation programs and policies.

16

New Ministries: Implications for Formation and Career Development

M. Vincentia Joseph, MSBT

In recent years apostolic Religious communities of women have experienced a changing or contingent character to some of their ministries, a result largely of the rapid rate of change as well as its scale and scope. No longer is it clear that the same types of work will be done in the same settings. Changes in ministry will be influenced increasingly by need, for need was the focus of the charismatic beginnings of apostolic congregations and must continue to be their focus if this form of Religious life is to be fully expressed today.

This presentation will focus on the implications of new ministries for formation programs and second careers. It will be made largely within a framework of social change and research on the roles of women Religious and priests. Prior to the Council there was little research in this area and since then only a few studies have been done. I will also draw on my own research on the role integration of the Sister social worker, which included all Religious professionally trained in social work at the Master's level in the United States since Vatican II. The specific focus was on the factors which influenced role integration, satisfaction, and conflict.[1] The study is applicable to Sisters in new and emerging ministries, since social work continues to be a marginal apostolate in most communities. The purpose of this paper is not to enumerate the various ministries but rather to consider some aspects of

114

our newer models which are relevant to socialization processes in communities — initial formation and on-going development.

As we know, there is a growing trend away from institutional settings to community and parish-based programs. Such settings have less structure and require greater skill in interpersonal relationships. Increasingly, ministries are concerned with individual and family life-cycle concerns; the rejected and alienated in society; and efforts to humanize societal institutions. Many Religious move into these areas without adequate preparation and supportive structures. Often they experience role ambiguity and isolation.

There is a growing need to incorporate into our ministries a futuristic orientation which seeks to identify trends for preventive and developmental planning. Innovation and creativity are required to discover viable solutions to problems. Because of the complexity of these problems, comprehensive team approaches are needed which value the expertise of the various fields of ministry and see them as reflecting essential aspects of the Church's mission. More and more, there is a demand for program evaluation and accountability.

In view of these trends, formation programs must be geared to the development of the self-directed person who can generate new service modalities and techniques for today's world as well as integrate the spiritual life with ministry. Adequate preparation for ministry is needed, especially when it is a second career. There was an overriding concern among the Sisters in my study over the number of Religious carrying out social work functions without training or direction.[2] There continues to be an attitude in many communities that no special training is needed for such work, a rejection of the specialized body of knowedge and skill developed by the profession.

Factors Influencing Role Performance and Religious Career Development

My research and that of others indicate that there are two major factors influencing the role performance of Religious: the person and the environment. The most significant variable in role satisfaction was self-role congruence (the fit between self and role), while the most powerful variable in role conflict was the organizational structure of Religious life.

Self-role congruence, the suitability of the person for the role, is especially pertinent to career development as it is significant both for work satisfaction and successful role integration. As in other studies, satisfaction with the work itself and the use of one's talents and abilities were central to role satisfaction. Most significant to role integration was the compatibility of the apostolic role with Religious life. It was interesting that less than one percent of the Sisters experienced conflict around the vow of celibacy, consistent with recent studies on the role of the priest. This may be related to the fact that the Sister social workers of the study were a high satisfaction group. Many writers suggest that conflict in this area may be the result of a more generalized role dissatisfaction.

Although communities are giving attention to career development, this area needs further consideration, especially as Sisters move into second careers. Over 80 percent of my study group had been in one or more occupations before selecting social work. Exactly half saw their pre-professional preparation for social work as inadequate and suggested that Sisters be given more opportunities to determine role suitability. The preferred form of screening-orientation modality and preparation for professional social work was experience in a professional setting.

Freedom of choice, although important, was not a sufficient factor in career selection — other variables were operating. Interestingly, those Sisters who had the greatest difficulty during their professional training in schools of social work experienced the greatest degree of role conflict later. This further indicates that organizational arrangements are needed to help Religious determine their suitability for a particular work. The data suggested that career decision-making is a process involving the Sister and her community made within a framework of: (1) personal choice; (2) role suitability; (3) communal goals; (4) apostolic needs.

Prior to the Council, the role conflict of Religious was rooted in a dualistic view of Religious life. Religious were caught between a bureaucratic model of Religious life, highly stylized and routinized, and the professional model with its humanistic value system. A pre-Vatican II study on Sister social workers identified a number of conflicts: some Religious were not permitted to go into certain neighborhoods or work with certain types of people; many were not permitted to do marriage counselling or attend meetings at night; community prayers often conflicted with work.[3] Surprisingly, as reported by over half of my study group (which represented 108 Religious congregations of women), these problems continue to exist to some degree. A number of communities still held that social work interfered with Religious life and brought too much contact with the secular, again reflecting a dichotomy of life and mission. Some Sisters experienced conflict around obedience, in expressing needs and preferences. I found, in a formation seminar on role integration, that several Sisters had questions in this area and needed help to see that stating occupational/professional preferences within a framework of obedience can actually enhance ministry.

According to my research, the most extensive conflict arising from "significant others" was other Religious, non-social workers, with whom the Sister lived. Consistent with other studies, a number experienced isolation, loneliness, and a sense of rejection. The group which was the second most extensive source of conflict to the Sisters was priests who were not social workers. The most *intensive* source of conflict, although it involved only a small group, was the Major Superior. This is especially significant in view of the changing role of the local superior.

Need to Intensify Efforts to Facilitate Expression of Person in Ministry

It seems clear from these data that greater efforts must be made to build community structures which reflect an understanding of the person especially as new/nontraditional roles are assumed. As Sisters who participated in my research urged, there needs to be a study of the theological base of the fields of ministry and how each of these is integrated in an over-all theology of mission.

Although the sociological literature generally suggests that role conflict is dysfunctional, more recently there has been evidence that it can be productive. Clearly, my study showed that it may be a negative experience or may be used positively. It may produce growth in both the person and the organization, depending on its management — the coping mechanisms utilized. This underscores the importance of creating environments which are supportive and encourage feedback.

Hall found that satisfaction was related to the type of coping strategy used.[4] Three types were defined: (1) environmental coping: external role demands are negotiated — that is, conflicting expectations for a particular role are dealt with directly; (2) personal role re-definition; personal expectations for the role are changed; (3) reactive coping: attempts are made to meet all demands or there is a passive response with no conscious strategy. Hall found that environmental strategies were the most satisfying while reactive coping was negatively related to satisfaction. It has been observed that Religious and priests frequently use reactive coping mechanisms to deal with role conflict, particularly passive-aggressive behaviors.[5] In view of these findings the following four-stage process model for coping with conflict should be useful to formation and on-going development: (1) a recognition of conflict; (2) the decision to cope; (3) an examination of one's personal role definition — at this stage role withdrawal may occur; (4) negotiating role demands/expectations directly with those involved.

The Religious woman, undoubtedly, will continue to assume new and varied roles in ministry, not only in response to changing needs but consistent with the restructuring of the roles of women in society. These roles may be viewed as newer expressions of the Church's mission in contemporary society. Karl Rahner refers to the secular professions and the emerging forms of ministry as modern, concrete models of the spiritual and corporal works of mercy. The Religious will, increasingly, take leadership roles within the framework of the Church and in the tradition of the ecclesial woman as long as community and church structures are viable and supportive of the vibrant movement taking place among Religious women in ministry. Our greatest challenge, perhaps, is to facilitate the authentic expression of the person in ministry throughout all phases of the life-span — from initial formation to entry into second careers during the middle and later phases of life. In our present state of knowledge, we are only beginning to understand the developmental possibilities and the rich potential for service at the latter phases. Every stage of the life process offers a unique contribution to ministry. Our efforts must be intensified to enhance the creative expression of each.

References

1.   Sister Mary Vincentia Joseph. "A Study of Self-Role Congruence and Role-Role Congruence on the Integration of the Religious Role and the Social Work Role of the Sister Social Worker." Unpublished DSW dissertation, The Catholic University of America, 1974. Three hundred twenty-three Religious professionally trained in social work during the period 1962-1972 (representing 108 communities) were located. The questionnaire response was 86.4%.

2.   Social work, the dominant or host profession in social service programs, prepares people for work with individuals, families, groups and communities.

3.   Sister Mary Brigid Fitzpatrick. "The Sister Social Worker: An Integration of Two Professional Roles." Unpublished Ph.D. dissertation, The University of Notre Dame, 1972.

4.   Douglas Hall. "A Model of Coping with Role Conflict: The Role Behavior of College Educated Women," *Administrative Science Quarterly*, 17 (December 1972), 471-86.

5.   Paul J. Weber and Sister Madeline Reno. "Conflict in Religious Communities: An Interview," *Review for Religious*, 33 (January 1974), 119-26.

Some Suggestions for Community Reflection on:

New Ministries: Implications for Formation and Career Development

- Which person or group in your community has the responsibility to identify what Sister Vincentia terms "trends for the kind of preventive and developmental planning" necessary in the area of ministry? Who is responsible for evaluation and accountability in the area of ministry? Who is responsible for adequate preparation of the Sisters for first, new, or second careers?
- The data suggests that career decision-making is a process involving the Sister and her community made within a framework of: (1) personal choice; (2) role suitability; (3) communal goals; (4) apostolic

needs. What has been your own personal as well as your community's experience with career decision-making in the last five years?

- Sister Vincentia stressed the need for future environments that are supportive and give encouraging feedback, as well as the need for coping mechanisms to deal with conflict. She presented a model which she felt would be helpful to formation personnel — a four-stage process model for coping with conflict. How is your community presently helping Sisters to adjust to any conflicts and difficulties they experience in assuming their new and non-traditional roles in ministry? What plans does the community have to better deal with such conflicts in the future?

- We are only beginning to understand the developmental possibilities and rich potential for service at the latter phases of the life-span. We sense that each stage of the life process offers a unique contribution to ministry. After reflecting quietly on your own ministerial experiences and the experiences of others in your community, share together what you think are the unique contributions of each age group. (Make sure there are Sisters of all ages present for the sharing.)

17

A New Look at
Formation for Mission

Caminante, no hay camino;
se hace camino al andar.
Antonio Machado
Traveller, there is no road;
the road is made by walking.

Ann Gormly, SNDdeN

There is need for a new theology and praxis of mission. In reflecting on a future-directed look at formation for mission, a number of preliminary points seem worth mentioning.

First of all, a distinction must be made between "mission" and "missions." The word "missions" usually referred to a place of apostolic endeavor in a culture other than one's own to which one was "sent" to "preach" the gospel. Today the validity of this understanding of the term is challenged. The Church, it is declared, is already present on all six continents: why be "sent"? Again, it is argued that the missionary is more appropriately "called" than sent. "Come" seems a more suitable missioning word than "go." Finally, many hold that the kind of proclamation that communicates clearly today is made through the witness of one's life; verbal proclamation or preaching is but secondary.

All these insights, partial as they are, provide glimpses into a wider synthesis of missionary vocation of the Christian. The call to serve the "missions" is a specification of a broader call to "mission," which is a constitutive element of the Church seen both as

121

"community of faith" and as "visible ecclesial structure" (*Lumen Gentium,* Art. 8). As such it is constitutive also of Religious communities.

Another distinction which must be made is that between "mission" and "ministry." Until fairly recently the mission to evangelize and the ministry or apostolic service undertaken were seen almost as coextensive. Schools for my foundress, for example, were "nets to catch souls" and when our older Sisters went to school in the morning, they were going "to save souls."[1] Today, we see *diakonia* as one aspect of evangelization and we question whether some forms of ministry that once were powerful witnesses may not today be counter-witnesses.

There is, finally, no single, inevitable future for which we are forming the young women who come to our congregations. The Spanish poet is right when he says that the road does not exist; that it is made by walking. But we can set out for a horizon to the left or the right of us, before us or behind our back. My few observations will not be applicable to every possible future, but I hope that some idea of the journey I envision us making can be grasped from the comments that follow. They center on two points: the need each person has for a personal theoretical understanding of mission; and the importance of seeing one's Religious life itself as mission, as witness to God's saving love for all.

Context: Reflection on Mission and World

If mission is constitutive of Religious communities, as it is of the Church, it is essential that each member, at whatever state of formation, be engaged in the dynamic process of developing a personal understanding of "mission." This understanding of mission must in turn be consistent with one's understanding of Church and salvation.

Many of us grew up in a world in which the ground of mission theology was Mark 16:15-16: "Go into the whole world and proclaim the good news to all creation. The man who believes in it and accepts baptism will be saved, the man who refuses to believe in it will be condemned." We tended to see salvation as normally coming through the Church. And it was the task or mission of the Church, and of us inserted in the Church, to go out and bring "souls" into the Church or go out and plant the Church and thus enlarge its presence in the world. Numbers were important and we were forever counting: baptisms, marriages, conversions. In our hospitals people would be able to die in the Church. Death was of extreme importance; to it and to the after-life, all was geared. In our schools children would be helped not to lose their faith and in the end die outside the Church.

In this view of mission God sent his son to redeem, to save humankind. This Son founded a Church and gave that Church a mission: to go to the ends of the world and bring the sheep into the fold.[2] For some this view is still credible; lifestyle or ministry decisions that are in harmony with it will, then, be understandable to candidates who subscribe to this theology.

Today, however, our understanding of the world presents real challenges to such a narrow view of Church and of mission. Candidates for Religious life should face these challenges. If they do not, they may find themselves making decisions about community life and service that are out of harmony with their theology. From this situation there can follow the loss of a sense of meaning.

A first challenge comes from a new view of history. Less than in the past are we Christians split into secular selves who know that human life goes back well over a million years and religious selves who see the Bible as the skeletal framework into which history is fitted. And so we can begin to ask: If the Church is only 2,000 years old and the human race perhaps two million, can salvation be only through the Church? Is not God's mission the salvation of *all* people in *all* times and places?

Another challenge we might call the "challenge of Asia." We know now that, after hundreds of years and large expenditure of financial and personnel resources, we are not going to convert great numbers of Muslims and Hindus and Buddhists. We were spoiled by early successes when we evangelized among people whose religion had little depth: the Greek world, Northern Europe. But Asia is very different. An understanding of Church built on numbers and expansion is meaningless, for example, in relation to China or India, with its highly developed Hindu culture that was able to absorb even a great religion like Buddhism.

Still another challenge comes to us from all parts of the world today, but it has been perhaps articulated theologically in Latin

America. That is the challenge of humanism. How has it happened that thousands have gone to Latin America to bring the good news, but actually have brought bad news: the message that God expects some to be very rich and others very poor; that if a person has to sleep on the Church steps while he lives, he can rejoice because his reward will be great in heaven. "Does God care for me *now?*" such a person will ask. "We cannot sit and spend long hours reading the gospel with cardinals, bishops, and pastors, all of whom are doing fine right where they are, while the flock wanders about in hunger and solitude," wrote the Bolivian Nestor Paz.[3] "The Gospel is not mechanical moralism," Paz says to the "priests of the established disorder, priests of the peace enforced by violence . . . of the complicity of silence . . . of pie in the sky when you die."[4]

Latin America today gives evidence on a massive scale that Church planting and "good news" proclamation are non-synonymous. The "missions" question may be "How announce God to the non-believer?" but the "mission" question becomes "How tell the non-person, the oppressed, wherever he is, that God is his Father and loves him?"

Formation for Mission: Asking the Right Questions

Present-day challenges to our view of mission, then, suggest to us that programs of formation must embrace the view that God's mission to the world is for the salvation, not only of the Church, but of the whole human community. What that mission looks like in the concrete can be seen in the way it was carried out by Jesus Christ. And as the Father sent him, so in turn he sends us. We begin to realize that instead of God's Church having a mission in the world, God's mission has a church in the world and that church is ourselves. Our task as church, and in a special way as Religious women, is to incarnate and give witness to God's saving love for all human persons.

To be this incarnation and witness in today's world, this leaven, what must our Religious life look like? How should we live and work in our world in a way that will be "good news," evangelizing? Surely our formation programs must be in view of this, our mission.

Just as the world situation can help us in the development of our theology of mission, so can it help us with the *praxis*. A daily reading of the front page of the paper, for example, will suggest that physical deprivation, powerlessness and alienation are the lot of most of the people in our world. The interrelatedness of each of these is fairly evident. Alienation is a consequence of both a lack of power and a lack of a sense of belonging. Deprivation of all material things is an accompaniment of third-class citizenship and a sign of the little worth of the powerless.

We hear not only individuals and groups but whole nations asking for a share in the goods of the earth. "Trade, not aid," they cry. They are not seeking a maternalistic/paternalistic share of our excess, the crumbs from our table, a downward-motion sharing, but rather a just return for the goods of their own land or the labor of their hands.

Such people recognize also that participation in decision-making that affects their lives is one of the major signs of power. New small nations, the so-called '77 at the U.N., have become aware of the strength that comes from having equal status around the bargaining table. People who lack this right to participate in decision-making, whose opinion is not even listened to, be they laity in the Church, farm workers in Brazil, or poor countries in a world controlled by global corporations, have little choice but apathy or violence.

Now in what sense is our life "good news" to such people? Surely Religious life is directly related to questions of powerlessness, poverty, and alienation. People will not ask if we express this relationship in vows, be they one or three. How we express it in our lives is what matters to them. Do our lives serve as signs of hope to the world? Does our celibate love reach out to the poor, lonely, and unimportant in a way that incarnates God's love for each of them? Do our decision-making structures demonstrate that each person's input has value, that each person should have a say in the matters that affect his or her life? What must our poverty look like for it to announce loud and clear that God is good? Will it mean greater personal renunciation; the forfeiting of institutional security? Can the sharing of corporate wealth be the answer? How will solidarity with the poor and oppressed be achieved by Religious congregations?

If our life is mission, then examining it is not a narcissistic endeavor. Mission is always in view of the other. Unless we listen carefully to the suffering of our brothers and sisters, unless they be, in some sense, part of our formation teams, we could be forming latter-day Pharisees.

In summary, then, formation today will require reflection on our personal and corporate life as mission. This reflection will have to be done in the context of our understanding of God's mission and in response to the challenges of the world we hope to evangelize.

References

1.   Cf. Sr. Mary Linscott, SNDdeN, *Religious Sisters and Evangelization Today* (USIG bulletin, 1st quarter 1975, no. 35) p. 15.
2.   Cf. 2 Tim. 1:9, 10; 1 Tim. 2:6.
3.   Nestor Paz, *My Life for My Friends*, trans. and ed. by Ed Garcia and John Eagleson (New York: Orbis, 1975) p. 22.
4.   *Ibid.*, p. 23.

Some Suggestions for Community Reflection on:

A New Look at Formation for Mission

- To move into the future, each Religious must be engaged in the "dynamic process of developing an understanding of mission consistent with one's understanding of Church and salvation." How is your community assisting its members in this process?
- A narrow view of Church and mission cannot support newer styles of community life and service. Such inconsistency between one's theology and one's practice eventually leads to the "loss of a sense of meaning." What are the effects of this on the individual Religious? on the community?
- What value do you see in current attempts to sensitize Religious to the cries of the poor? Share what your community has done in this regard through formative experiences, programs.
- Are formation personnel asking the right questions about the vowed life — the incarnation of the good news in a lifestyle that speaks to people today? What are your questions about the vowed life in apostolic communities of the future?

18

What Direction Health Ministries: Pushing Out the Walls

Margaret Ebbing, SC

Religious have always looked upon health ministry as a major form of service. For decades, thousands of Religious Brothers and Sisters have given health care within the walls of Catholic hospitals and institutions.

After thirty years of service within such walls, I set out for Africa at the age of fifty and discovered that my entry into the third world made the whole world shrink. Any description I might attempt would fall short of the reality. In Africa, I quickly became familiar with the horrors of human degradation and learned firsthand those diseases that had till then been only textbook knowledge. Africa is a nation that has borne the burden of centuries of suffering. I learned that preventive medicine, the future thrust in health care, is unavailable not only to many in the United States but also to most in Africa.

Health Ministry Outside the Walls

When I returned to the United States in 1974, having learned lessons for the future that only the poor sick can teach, I chose to serve without the walls. My ministry at East Coast Migrant Projects is but one example of a service-oriented career available to Religious who wish to direct their devotion to the poor sick in new ways. I see the future of the health ministry as now being outside the walls of our institutions. In the past, health workers focused

127

upon cure; tomorrow they must focus upon prevention. Hospital planning boards, encouraged by state and county boards, are looking in new directions because programs such as the East Coast Migrant Projects have uncovered pockets of total neglect. They have discovered that thousands of forgotten Americans are not obtaining even the health care that is presently available.

It is estimated that there are 1.5 million migrant/seasonal agricultural farmworkers and their families who travel up and down the Eastern coast harvesting fruits and vegetables. For their "stoop labor" they reap no benefits, and barely subsist on their small salaries.

Religious as Change Agents

Since 1970, the East Coast Migrant Projects have received funding from the Department of Health, Education, and Welfare although the staff is sponsored by the Leadership Conference of Women Religious. The components of the projects are now health care, preschool education, and social services. These services are extended at the invitation of the migrant-impacted counties.

In addition to voicing a desire for this involvement, participating counties work closely with the staff of ECMP in locating, mobilizing, and/or providing local resources. Clinical facilities, physician services, and auxiliary workers for mutual support are essential in translating intention into reality. Our long-term goal is to make health care services known and available to the migrant.

The migrant for varying reasons has espoused an atypical lifestyle. Reasons include such things as: birth into a migratory family; personal choice; societal disenchantment; lack of family support; high levels of unemployment; and inadequate vocational and/or educational preparation. Our staff perceives the migratory lifestyle as isolated and disenfranchised. It is our intention to serve as a change agent in improving a lifestyle which, as it now generally exists, is rightly considered undesirable and degrading. Our hope is that some day migrants will be able to become part of the society that has closed them out.

My role is to recruit laborers for health ministry in the fields. I can only tell you what it *looks* like to be deprived, but not what it *feels* like. "I have come that you might have life and have it more fully." The Religious of the future in health ministry must hear these words of Jesus and bring life to all, but especially those migrating on the fringes of the society.

New Skills Needed for the Future

Let me now focus on the caliber of person needed for health ministry outside the walls of our institutions. If the letters I receive for service with our projects are an indication of the service-conviction of our youth, we are blessed. One woman writes: "I feel that the type of work you have done and the issues you have been concerned with are important. I would like to know if you are open to the possibility of having someone whose basic focus coincides with your own, to come to work with you?"

The applicant continues, "I think my résumé indicates that I believe it is imperative to work on improving the present health care system. From my own experience and from what I have seen in my community and in the community in which I live, I believe that the present system is inadequate and to a large extent unresponsive to the needs of the people it is supposed to be serving. I have done fundraising and have worked to solicit the support of community leaders for the development of health care facilities which I believed would better the quality and increase the availability of health care in the area. Although I have become aware of the complexities of the economic, social and political systems that one must work through to implement change, I remain committed to working in this direction."

Such applicants are graduates of new health programs — health associates from the Johns Hopkins program, physician assistants of Yale, specialists in pediatrics, maternal and child care, cardiology and emergency care. They want to be part of health care services where there is none.

Religious Life Outside the Walls

There are many implications for the future in pushing out the walls of our health structures. Future health ministers must have the ability to live in small groups and to find recreational opportunities in the bush or field areas far from the cities. They must know how to surmount creatively the frustrations of working in poor areas. One of our Sisters who has just returned from serving in a bush clinic in Ecuador exchanged ideas with me. She feels that Religious life in the future will be marked by a simplicity of lifestyle, a deep prayer life, small group living, and a presence among the people one is serving. Since work with the poor is so draining, Religious in health ministries of the future must not only be well formed but also able to continue their own on-going formation. New primary health care givers are trained for service outside the walls. They would be underused in institutions where expertise is concentrated.

While I was preparing my observations I felt the need to correspond with a modern prophet concerning her ideas on the Religious of the future. Jeane Dixon's message for Religious of the future was: "Seek what is permanent." She sees the Religious resurgence of the 1980s as a signal for a return to prayer and poverty. I also wrote to Mother Teresa of Calcutta. She responded in a similar vein. She wrote, "The most important element for all of us today is the conviction that we belong to Christ and that he has chosen us for himself. To be able to live up to that conviction, we need a life of poverty and of prayer. I say poverty first, because poverty is freedom. Through this freedom, we are able to be completely one with Christ in prayer and to share his passion and so redeem the world with him."

Let me summarize by saying:

- Health care and hospitals will always be provided for those who can afford to pay. Progress in technology will continue, as will the demand for sophisticated methods and highly-trained personnel.

- The poor who have not had health care have waited long enough. Forces, political and humane, will surge to bring about health education and preventive care for the masses.

- Practical health givers such as the primary Nurse Practitioners, Health Associates, and Nurse Clinicians will abound. They will not only provide the first-line care through screening and referral, but will stabilize the tide of disease through prompt detection.

- Religious will be valued and active as first-line health givers. They have the availability needed to work in outlying districts. Travel and broad exposure will increase their concern for their brothers and sisters in the third and fourth worlds.

- Religious life will develop in small groups nourished by a deep spiritual life and sustained by mutual support.
- Religious will live in numerous intercommunity settings in which many personal and community charisms will come together and blend in a beautiful mosaic. Religious will experience anew St. Elizabeth Seton's challenge to "Be daughters of the Church."

Pushing out the walls of our institutions will enable health ministers to say with the author of the Japanese haiku, "Since my house burned down, I now own a new view of the rising moon."

Some Suggestions for Community Reflection on:

What Direction Health Ministries: Pushing Out the Walls

- What "third world" experiences has your community provided so that its members can experience new or different cultures?
- What have been the results of attempts by communities to raise the consciousness of Religious to the real needs of those in need of healing?
- How are the members of your community presently experiencing themselves as healers in traditional ministries? in new forms of ministry?
- How would you envision the Church in health ministries in the future?
- How will the ordination of women affect the healing ministries in the Church?

19

Models of Formation:
An African Frame of Reference

Mary Shawn Copeland, OP

It is rooted in the human personality to know one's self fully — as fully as one can — to know especially from where and from whom one has come. This knowledge eases the journey forward; this is wholeness, and hence the beginning of holiness.

Liberation is a mutual process whereby persons or a people are freed. The goal of the several and varying revolutions occurring in the world in this century is liberation. Indigenization is the agonizing, anxious, and satisfying struggle of people to reassume control of their lives and the future of their children. It is to recreate and expand their collective history — to write and to direct the new drama — to select the new actors and challenge the former denouement. This critical resumption of cultural conformation develops identity and spills over into the political sphere. It puts to route economic and political institutional and/or systemic oppression and control. It grasps the necessity for engaging in the cre/action of change.

There can be no political liberation which does not assume the liberation of the spirit. The liberation of the body politic frequently illuminates the dubious religious philosophy which has been exercised to manipulate the populace psychologically and to entrench the oppressors.

The African Setting

Especially in Africa has all this been felt. Africa: where to live is to be caught up in a religious drama. The African world is a religious world. Persons are seen to be deeply religious beings living in a religious world. This world and nearly all of a person's activities in it are perceived and experienced through religious significance.

There is no doubt that African religious thought is essentially *theocentric* and *theistic*. "God" is at the center of it all. This is not to say that it is either monotheistic or polytheistic.[1] Rather to be (in African understanding) is to be religious in a religious universe. This is the philosophical understanding behind African myths, customs, traditions, beliefs, morals, actions, and social relationships.

Religion within the context of traditional African life is exceedingly difficult to define. It can best be described as an *ontological phenomenon*; it pertains to the question of existence or being. In this universe, names of people have religious connotations; mountains, rocks, water, are not just *objects*, but religious objects; the drum is an instrument of speaking a holy/religious language. There are innumerable examples, but the point is that for Africans, the whole of existence is a religious phenomenon.

The ontology of the African is an *anthropocentric ontology*. *Anthropocentric ontology* places the human person at the center with God as the originator and sustainer; animals, plants, natural phenomena and objects comprise the environment in which the human person lives. This ontology is characterized by a completeness and unity which cannot be destroyed or broken. To destroy one or remove one is to destroy the whole existence.[2]

This *anthropocentric ontology* was communally organized; persons lived in community, relationships with God were communally structured. There was a marked interdependence of person, God and nature.

This ontology experiences a mutually supportive and influential role in "traditional" African culture. "Traditional" African culture is that African culture (tribal, communal, varying and specific) as it appeared prior to the mid-1800s and 1945. This "traditional" culture had deep roots in the countless centuries of civili-

zation that preceded it and it furnished much of the substance
and idiom of the new Africa.[3]

Christianity and modern change are *interventions* in this ontology and in the traditional African culture. The late Kwame Nkrumah writes:

> African society has . . . a segment which represents the infiltration of
> the Christian tradition and culture of Western Europe into Africa,
> using colonialism and neocolonialism as its primary vehicles.[4]

Yet, Christianity continues to be a paradox. John S. Mbiti tells
us in *African Religions and Philosophy* that the uniqueness of
Christianity is not in its teaching, practice, or ritual and rubrics;
rather this uniqueness lies in Christ Jesus. He is the stumbling
block of all ideologies and theological systems. His own Person is
greater than can be contained in any particular religion or ideology. He is the "Man for others" and the Man beyond them. This
Christ, fully human and hence fully divine/religious, continuing,
and timeless: this is what Christianity can offer beyond, and in
spite of, "its own anachronisms and divisions in Africa."[5]

Religion/Christianity must have a greater role to play in present-day Africa than simply supplying new myths or reviving old
ones. It ought and can provide tools and challenge and inspiration
for a rethinking and response to the basic issues of our time.

Mbiti writes further:

> The final test for the continuing existence of these religions in our
> continent is not which one shall win in the end. The test is whether
> mankind benefits or loses from having allowed religion to occupy
> such a privileged and dominating position in human history, in
> man's search for his origin and nature of being, in the experience of
> responding to his environment, and in the creation of his expecta-
> tions and hope for the future.[6]

Such a "test" might appropriately be applied to the presence of
Religious congregations — both indigenous and nonindigenous,
both in Africa and in the United States — and may be applied to
the philosophy of Religious formation.

What surfaces immediately in reflecting upon Mbiti's challenge is the implicit reference to ministry: whether humankind
benefits (is served adequately and appropriately) or loses from the
presence of women who are called "Sister," and that the search of
human persons for *truth* is forged in a dynamic dialectic.

Formation then is not necessarily successful because all the candidates remain in community, but rather it is successful when each candidate pursues a personal origin and the nature of that personal *call*; when each candidate is in search of the experience(s) of responding to a personal environment; and in the creation of personal expectations and hope for her future and the future of the candidate's people.

For our purposes, the diagram (Fig. 1) is seen as a self-explanatory working-schema for highlighting germane concepts for the organizing of formation. Such a diagram is not reflective of the highly creative tensions present and so necessary for the growth of new models.

The Basic Theses

Preliminary to the theses for organizing the formation model are the following: 1) the basic attitudes of respect and listening; 2) an awareness of the complexity and depth of the struggle black (*Afro*American) Religious women must encounter to live and work, and be in Africa; 3) an appreciation of formation as that personal inner-dynamic which compels a generous creative response to God's action in one's life, and to the gospel imperative to become a reconciling agent in the transformation of the world.

Such preliminary assumptions prepare us for these basic theses.

1. The role of the Religious congregation/the Religious must be submerged in the historical process.

2. It is the responsibility of the Religious congregation/the Religious to participate in the transformation of the world in which they find themselves at that period in history.

3. Religion and politics are inevitable dimensions of human life.

4. Spirituality is bounded and conditioned, enhanced and strengthened, developed and explained by culture and history.

An exploration of these theses will clarify the diagram.

Figure 1. Formation Models

Dimension	European Models	Reformist Models	New Models
Goals	Visual Institutional Measurable	Inclusion In Present Structure	Christian Commitment to Struggles of Peoples
Authorities	European: Superior-Subject	Euro-trained: Election of Superiors	Indigenous: Collegiality, Subsidiarity
Theological Orientation	Post-Vatican II Development of new laws (Structured Prayers)	Vatican II Development of New Structure (Spontaneous Prayer)	Vatican II Development of New Spirit Serious Questions of Mission, Ministry, Political Theology, Political Ecclesiology (Interiorized Prayer)
Identity/Culture	European	Transitional (Re-discovery)	Indigenous
Ministerial Philosophy	Missionizing	Co-operative	Co-terminus (Discerned by/with served and serving)

The role of the Religious congregation/the Religious must be submerged in the historical process.

The Religious congregation and Religious develop in a particular place, at a particular time, in the face of particular needs. The congregation cannot escape from or ignore the fundamental message of the gospel — that God is plunged irrevocably in the midst of human history. It is this vivid memory which must never pale.

Jesus challenged his world. He sacramentalized commitment for the transformation of that world/commitment for the sake of the kingdom. He took responsibility for his world and for his life in the world. He was present to people by his prophetic role and by his discernment. He was called *out of the community for service by the times*, by the needs and by the history of his people; called out only to return.

It is the responsibility of the Religious congregation/the Religious to participate in the transformation of the world in which they find themselves at that period in history.

Liberation is not achieved in a vacuum, nor solely in the personal forum; rather it is forged in the thick of the struggle and in collective, as well as individual, acceptance of responsibility for working toward a world which reflects values that are human and communal and loving. Religious must engage in the assessment of needs and in the reflection and in the design of mechanisms of imagination and value which provide opportunities for participation in changing reality.

How is this different from previous "historial commitment" by Religious congregations? In this manner: quite simply, the congregation is captive of the gospel, the gospel is no longer captive of the Religious congregation.

Religion and politics are inevitable dimensions of human life.

One cannot be alive and not have such affiliations. The eschatological promise (the prevision of the kingdom) — freedom, peace, justice, reconciliation — are not private promises, they are public. Hence we must seek to live out those promises in the "now" in order to insure the establishment of the kingdom. No political machine or device can espouse the radical virtues — faith, hope and love. Faith seeks to draw us to the past, remembered and renewed. Hope delivers us from a monolithic view of governments and history; it centers us for the future. Love/charity is not merely an interpersonal, social affair; rather it is that which resolves us to seek freedom, work for peace, establish justice and live in an attitude of reconciliation.

While God is at one with us as to the righteousness of our struggle, he will not liberate us/establish the kingdom without our purposeful, intelligent and human activity. It is vital that Religious be unafraid of the political. Jesus was political; his continued preaching about liberation and the coming of a kingdom earned him crucifixion — a political execution.

Africans — both on the continent and in the diaspora — are actively engaged in operations (military, paramilitary, rhetorical, philosophical) against forces of reaction and counterrevolution. Africans still suffer the "political" effects of capture, slavery, dehumanization, colonization, neocolonization.

Religious clearly have responsibilities with regard to their peoples' oppression.

All spirituality is bounded and conditioned, enhanced and strengthened, developed and explained by culture and history.

Indigenous Religious have the responsibility, the privilege, to free and possess their spirituality by seizing their culture. Thus, the "formation" of the "Sister" who is servant of the people must be governed by objectives and values springing from her culture.

Generative themes of prayer are revealed and nourished. Such themes as remembrance, communion, fidelity, aloneness, creation, experience, communication, organization culminate in participation, so that

> . . . participation . . . once an imposed necessity, has become an art of sharing, an attitude of listening . . . which challenge us continually . . . (van Kaam)

From Theses to Process

In reference to the Benin-Model, these theses find application in the following manner:

- An environment is created, an atmosphere facilitated, wherein a process is given to problem-solving. The resolution/understanding of the problem is achieved by the learner.

- The model for developing a spiritual life is found in the person of Christ through the gospel.
- Values taught and values lived are struggled into harmony so as to create more credibility for modern Religious life as it is institutionalized.
- Training is not done in alienation. Its curriculum is geared toward the needs and interests of a developing ministry.
- Maximum identity reinforcement is established with the introduction of key formation personnel who are Nigerian, AfroAmerican.
- The "communal" Religious life reflects the life of the wider Nigerian (Uromi) society. (The *novices* "market" on market days; farm; attend Mass with people of village, etc.)

The AfroAmerican Setting

To speak about developing a black methodology for the formation of Religious women is not simply a matter of focusing on a different problematic. To speak of a unique and contemporary black process for Religious formation is to accept and validate a distinct black cultural/spiritual experience in the United States.

Let us begin by reviewing our basic theses. Briefly, then:

- The Religious must be submerged in the historical process.
- It is the responsibility of the Religious to participate in the transformation of the world in which they find themselves at a given period of history.
- Religion and politics remain inevitable dimensions of human life and critical dimensions for oppressed and colonized persons.
- Culture and history continue to shape spirituality.

At least one preliminary can be added to previous assumptions: that blackness is a dynamic inherent in the values, attitudes, orientations, and genius of people of African descent living in the United States. It is an ambience, a milieu, and a force; and it is positive and a challenge. This last preliminary requires some discussion of the basis of blackness: *color, culture* and *consciousness*.

The three criteria for culture are *awareness, acceptance,* and *practice*. Culture cannot "happen" unless there is a control of the internal and external mechanisms that instill culture. To instill the three ends of culture — that is, *identity, purpose* and *direc-*

tion — a structure, a plan, and a system or enterprise to enforce and regulate the plan is required.[7]

Identity, purpose and direction yield a consciousness that manifests itself through a black value system.[8] Such a value system must cope with the reality of black women and men living in the United States; it must be rational and modern enough in its American orientation to deal with the socio-economics of our society, and yet not reflect that society. Such a value system ought to challenge that society and offer black women and men new guidelines for changing the contours of their lifestyle, art, economics, politics and more.

Within this context, it seems appropriate to reflect on the role of the black nun in America.

The call to Religious life comes from God and is offered to many and diverse people. Christ calls the person to follow him — in joy and in sorrow; to pick up the cross and walk in a new road, often difficult but not cheerless.

This call coming to a black woman is different in its theological anthropology than it is for a white woman. It is the *theological anthropological setting* which effects this difference. The white woman moves from her father's and mother's house into a setting which supports her racial anthropology and usually her cultural anthropology. The black woman is "called" from her father's and mother's house into a setting which is antithetical to her racial and cultural theology and anthropology. The black woman "leaves" her family and must establish new "familial" ties with a people who have been centuries-hostile to her family and her family's people.

Like Abraham, the black woman entering Religious life embarks upon a journey that is faith-ed. Like Ruth, she makes a "foreign" people her own and gleans among alien corn to sow and reap a new harvest. Like Esther, the black woman entering Religious life must be in a constant communication with her people, ever conscious of the power of (t)he(i)r presence to those who are not yet sensitive to (t)he(i)r story and need.

The "call" the black woman Religious experiences is in demand of commitment, consciousness, and action. This call reaches deep into the very marrow of her bones and the fiber of her soul.

Her "role" is well described through the prophet Jeremiah (20:7-9) for her word is a difficult one to live and speak:

> You have seduced me, Yahweh, and I have
> let myself be seduced;
> you have overpowered me: you were the
> stronger.
> I am a daily laughing-stock,
> everybody's butt.
> Each time I speak the word, I have to
> howl
> and proclaim: 'Violence and ruin!'
> The word of Yahweh has meant for me
> insult, derision, all day long.
> I used to say, 'I will not think about him,
> I will not speak in his name any more.'
> Then there seemed to be a fire burning
> in my heart,
> imprisoned in my bones.
> The effort to restrain it wearied me,
> I could not bear it.

From Theses to Process

Blackness is not valued in general in our society and a growing number of black women and men consciously document the United States government's attitude toward its dark skinned citizens as hostile. In *The Choice*, Sam Yette argues a strong case for the possibility of the extermination of "obsolete" black women and men.

For a woman whose people, in the opinion of many, face a growing and serious threat of death by genocide, engagement in critical tasks which aim at the survival of black people is important. Such a woman cannot, must not, will not dedicate months/years to minutiae.

The liberation/political theology which speaks from the vantage of *blackness* to *Religious life* declares that

- the vowed/communal life is relevant to and for the black community, *if* delivered and controlled by that community
- the challenge emanating from blackness can only be met by a formation program which develops the "collective woman," a program which

1) develops the black woman as an effective agent of the liberation of black people . . .
2) develops a leadership capable of systematic and innovative problem-solving and skilled behavior . . . and
3) provides an atmosphere conducive to introspection which enables black women to participate in and strengthen and develop spiritual and empirical awareness so as to believe and act, as Sojourner Truth, that the "power of a nation is within us. . . ."

In references to a Black (United States) Model, the theses would find application as indicated in Table 1. This assumes that the director of formation is structurally involved with the National Black Sisters Conference.

Conclusion

My concluding comments will be more of a statement for the black (American) model than the Benin-model as it is my judgment that a more explicit interpretation is required.

The postulation of a distinctly black methodology for formation in the United States is a "political" question. The "introduction" of black women into a particular formation program as into a particular Religious congregation is also a "political" question. These are political questions because as we meditate/contemplate on theology, we are confronted with the policy of the Church we serve and form and the policy of vocation.

We know that the task of creating new *directive images*, of discarding old definitions and redefining values is not as difficult nor as impossible as we once believed. Paradigms exist as they always have: women like Harriet Tubman, Sojourner Truth, and Mary McCleod Bethune (as well as Marcus Garvey, Fredrick Douglass) and others.

We know that traditions and institutions, whether positive or negative, can and do order and form the natural energies of a person or people. Energy can, as well, re-order, re-design traditions and institutions. The energy of black women needs must be channelled for the survival of her people.

History, tradition, and institutions require that black women Religious be whole women, women who have strong personal identity, women capable of decision-making and self-determina-

Table 1
Director of Formation
(structurally involved with NBSC)

Periodic Interaction:

Initiates, Affiliates (those women "formally" contemplating entrance and in structured contact with the congregation)

• periodic interaction with black Religious women (correspondence, visits, personal conversation, retreat/prayer experiences)

• participation in "work/living" experience with black Religious women

Candidates (those women who have "formally" entered a Religious congregation, but are not in "novitiate" stage), and more regular interaction with black Religious women (emphasis on reflection and discussion, possible situation for shared ministry, i.e., working in situation where black Sisters are employed; retreat/prayer experiences)

Regular Sessions:

of input/reflection involving candidates and black Religious women (such a program would move themes through a socio-politico-historical dynamic, a psychological dynamic, a theological dynamic and result in *praxis* [prayer, worship, work/action/response], reinforced by possible summer work experience structured by NBSC

Novitiate: The canonical year is still accepted as a "year apart"; it is not accepted as a year of isolation. The canonical year should set a "model," if you will, for living, not stand as an antithesis to it.

Black Religious women ought continue to be directly involved in the formation program throughout this *entire* period. Their presence provides a *reenforcing directive image.*

This year ought facilitate the personal development of the individual novice. The entire novitiate is to be an exploration — intellectual and spiritual — into the nature and meaning of Religious life and the personal application of that nature and meaning.

tion; they must as well be women whose vision is gospel-commitment and whose low investment in societal values allows her to live with risk.

Essential ingredients of a black methodology for formation
- must include mechanisms for maximum development of a meaningful sense of identity with the past and future . . .
- must include productive activity, in which young women choose tasks and participate in implementation, evaluation, modification . . .
- must include opportunity for increased political consciousness and "justice-d" responsibilities. Such opportunities are linked with "struggle" — the acquisition of understanding, of knowledge, the freedom of thought and challenge, the freedom of accountability so readily seen in the gospel imperative.

Perhaps it is time for a story:

There is a black folk tale . . . a story which happened long, long ago, at a time when black people were snatched from their homes in Africa and forced to come to America as slaves. They were put onto ships, and many died during the long voyage across the Atlantic Ocean.

Those who survived stepped onto a land they had never seen, a land they never knew existed, and they were put into the fields to work. Many refused and they were killed. When some were whipped, they turned to fight: some killed the white men who whipped them, some were killed by the white men. Some would run away trying to go back to Africa.

On a plantation in South Carolina, one boatload of Africans included the son of a witch doctor who had completed, but not by many months, studying the secrets of the gods under his father. This young man carried with him the secrets and powers of the generations of Africa.

One day when the sun had nearly singed the very hair on the heads of black folk working in the fields, a young black woman, full with child, fainted.

The overseer threw water in her face and ordered her back to work. He cracked a whip against her back.

All work stopped as the Africans watched, saying nothing. With the overseer's threat, the people went back to work.

The young witch doctor worked his way to the side of the stag-gering young woman and whispered something in her ear. She, in turn, whispered to the person beside her. He told the next person, and on around the field it went. They did it so quickly and quietly that the white overseer with the whip noticed nothing.

A few moments later, someone else in the field fainted and, as the white overseer with the whip rode toward him, the young witch doctor shouted, "Now!" He uttered a strange word, and the person who had fainted rose from the ground. Moving his arms like wings, he flew into the sky and out of sight.

The overseer looked around at the Africans but they only looked at the sky. "Who did that? Who was that who yelled out?" No one answered.

Soon a young woman fainted. The overseer was almost upon her when the young witch doctor shouted, "Now!" and uttered a strange word. She, too, rose from the ground and, waving her arms like wings, flew into the distance and out of sight.

This time the man with the whip knew who was responsible, and as he pulled back his arm to lash the young witch doctor, the young man yelled, "Now! Now! Everyone!" He uttered the strange word, and all of the Africans dropped their hoes, stretched out their arms, and flew away, back to their home, back to Africa.

That was long, long ago, and no one now remembers what word it was that the young witch doctor knew that could make our people fly. But who knows? Maybe one morning someone will awake with a strange word on her/his tongue and, uttering it, we will all stretch out our arms and take to the air, leaving these blood-drenched fields of our misery behind.

Some people will balk at such a "story," calling it too poetical, too fictitious for the purposes of discussing models of formation. But this is what we are fundamentally all about: struggling to re-cover our lost powers of flight — flight in the deepest sense of that word. . . . A flight that will not take us beyond earthly grav-ity, but a flight that will take us beyond the gravity of cruel insti-tutions, mindless oppression, and calloused structures. . . . A flight that will take us over limiting horizons and dense clouds and into a land not so much promised but promising.

References

1. Peter Sarpong, *Ghana in Retrospect* (Accra: Ghana Publishing Corporation, 1974), *passim*; pp. 9-13 in particular.

2. John S. Mbiti, *African Religions and Philosophy* (New York: Doubleday & Company, Inc., 1970), *passim*; pp. 19-23 in particular.

3. Paul Bohannan, *Africa and Africans* (New York: The Natural History Press, 1964), p. 239.

4. Kwame Nkrumah, *Consciencism* (London: Monthly Review Press, 1970), p. 68.

5. Mbiti, *op. cit.*, p. 363.

6. *Ibid.*, p. 363.

7. Don. L. Lee (Haki R. Madhubuti), *From Plan to Planet* (Detroit: Broadside Press, 1973), p. 47.

8. Cf. *Ibid.*, p. 80. (Reference is made to the *Nguzo Saba* or Black Value System as delineated by Ron Karenga and listed herein.)

Further Reading

James A. Banks, and Jean D. Grambs, Eds., *Black Self-Concept* (New York: McGraw-Hill Book Company, 1972.

Leonard E. Barrett, *Soul-Force* (New York: Pres/Doubleday, 1974).

C. Daniel Baston, *Commitment Without Ideology* (Philadelphia: United Church Press, 1973).

Lerone Bennett, Jr., *The Challenge of Blackness* (Chicago: Johnson Publishing Company, Inc., 1972).

James H. Cone, *A Black Theology of Liberation* (Philadelphia: Lippincott, 1970).

James H. Cone, *Black Theology and Black Power* (New York: Seabury Press, 1969).

W. E. B. DuBois, *The Souls of Black Folk* (Greenwich, Connecticut: Fawcett Publications, Inc., 1961).

Frantz Fanon, *A Dying Colonialism*, Trans. Haakan Chevalier (New York: Grove Press, Inc., 1967).

Frantz Fanon, *The Wretched of the Earth*, Trans. Constance Farrington (New York: Grove Press, Inc., 1967).

Vittorio Lanternari, *The Religions of the Oppressed*, Trans. Lisa Sergio (New York: The New American Library, Inc., 1965).

Don L. Lee, *Directionscore* (Detroit: Broadside Press, 1971).

Joseph R. Washington, Jr., *The Politics of God* (Boston: Beacon Press, 1970).

Sidney M. Willhelm, *Who Needs the Negro?* (New York: Doubleday & Company, Inc., 1971).

Henry Winston, *Strategy for a Black Agenda* (New York: International Publishers, 1973).

Samuel F. Yette, *The Choice* (New York: G. P. Putnam's Sons, 1971).

Johari M. Amini, *An African Frame of Reference*, Institute of Positive Education (1972).

Charles Cobb, *African Notebook: Views on Returning Home*, Institute of Positive Education (1972).

Mary Shawn Copeland, *"What Can Third World Religious Teach Us About the Future,"* an unpublished address given at Bergamo Center, June 1975.

Vincent M. Harding, "Towards A Black Theology," *Black Survival: Past — Present — Future*, pp. 69-78.

Dominic M. Mwasaru, "Where to Begin? Moving Towards Adequate Ministry," *AFER* (African Ecclesiastical Review, Vol. 17, No. 1, January 1975), pp. 9-17.

Julius Nyerere, Address to the Maryknoll Sisters Ninth General Assembly, 16 October 1970 (an unpublished paper).

Eskine Peters, "The Grounds and Our Minds: Notes Toward Understanding and Freeing" (an unpublished paper) Spring, 1975.

Bishop J. Sangu, "Special Concerns of Evangelization in Africa: Document for 1974 Synod of Bishops," *AFER* (Vol. 17, No. 1, January 1975), pp. 43-49.

Some Suggestions for Community Reflection on:

Models of Formation:
An African Frame of Reference

- What have you and your community done to encourage and forward black women in your area? to encourage and foster black vocations?
- At the present time, could a black woman in your community grow as a black woman? Are black Sisters encouraged and free to work with their own people?
- Are the formation personnel in your community willing to learn from and cooperate with the National Black Sisters Conference in creating models for formation?
- Using the guidelines presented by Sister Shawn in her paper, how would you see yourself working together with a black Sister in formation so that her formation program would be formative both for her and for your total community?
- How do you feel about Sister Shawn's statement: "The 'introduction' of black women into a particular formation program or into a particular Religious congregation is a 'political' question?"

20

The Culturally Advantaged Sister: Implications for Total Community Formation

Maria Iglesias, SC

It is probable that somewhere in our past we can recall a question that we learned the answer for in our very early formation as a child, "Why did God make us?" Our memories are strong and quite clear, and we can almost hear sixty or so baby voices saying loud and in not too great unison, "God made us to know, love and serve him in this world and to be happy with him in the next." Our experience of Church in 1975 is perhaps very far removed from this type of evangelization, and yet it was part of the reflections that led to the writing of this paper.

It seems to me that perhaps the fundamental advantage a Sister has who brings to her congregation a culture that is quite different either from the one most of the women who are members possess or from what some persons would term "American" is that she has an edge on "knowing" a people, a race, a minority or majority group from within. Today there are several theologians who are highlighting for us the implications that the mystery of Jesus' Incarnation has on formation. Jesus the teacher came and became "one of" his pupils. The Lord revealed the Father from within a race, a nation, a culture. As missionologists have begun to realize, more and more the "Good News" is present everywhere; it is for the Christian to be the catalyst for its discovery.

Only then does it become truly salvation for anyone.

The minister is not someone "set apart" anymore. She is someone who is heart, soul, and mind in a community, knowing and living its joys and pains, its hopes and fears, its burdens and resources. She (because we are talking of Sisters) loves the people deeply and effects change through this powerful commitment.

When a human being experiences being loved it is closely tied to whether or not I believe you know me. We witness many tragedies in human relationships when it is discovered that as knowledge grows, love diminishes. As a consequence our society has grown to distrust words and promises of love. It is here that the mystery of Jesus' gift to us of reconciliation has its strongest power to heal: when a person realizes that he or she is known in their weakness as well as their strength and is still loved.

Total Community Formation: Process of Knowing and Loving

Part of these reflections are also fruit of my experience in Religious life. I entered a community in which the ethnic and cultural background of the majority of Sisters was different from my own family. These same Sisters had been my teachers since I was six years old, and much of the cultural enrichment of my schooling was from them. I attribute to this factor the reason for my early perseverance in the community and why I had a certain "at home" feeling. In fact, later on in Religious life I was able to "teach" Sisters in my age group, from the same cultural background as the "older" Sisters, the songs and dances of their culture.

Looking back now, I believe it said effectively, "See how I love you and know you, I can sing and dance like your grandmother and mother." Some psychoanalysts can have a lot of comments to make perhaps, but a very old quotation from the past echoes in my mind right now. Those who have experienced being "in love" realize with surprise that it is operating in themselves: "imitation is the highest form of praise."

Jesus' love was radical; he who is God wants to be just like me in everything except sin! It seems that this level of loving is what we are about if we are to be Jesus for my sister or my brother.

Many Religious have known from their early novitiate days a struggle when their "love" was measured by how closely they imitated the Rule. Now we see how this artificial imitation never led too many Sisters to effective love. It was far easier to imitate the people nearest to them, and many a Sister could be identified by the mannerisms of a particular novice mistress! The principle that much of the curriculum of formation programs was formulated on was that the new members must get to know the ideal of the congregation so that they could dedicate their lives in imitation. Much more can be said and studied in this whole area of human life, since it ties in to the mandate of the Lord to love.

The People Reveal the Meaning of Vocation

In my own life an assignment was the vehicle for a new awakening. I was sent to work among the ethnic group my own family came from, and I came to them an extremely poor woman. The songs, the dances, the human expressions of my own ancestors were "foreign" to me. Even the language was hard, due to non-use for practically all of my formation from age six. Greater was the shock when the very Sisters and priests who "trained" me expressed a certain amount of scorn and disappointment that I was unable to teach them the culture of "my" people.

My salvation came from the people who helped me reach a deep level of understanding of my Religious vocation as "their" sign of faith as well as "God's sign." We witness that God can and will work in the lives of human beings and that this is all a free gift.

Open Communities Realize Jesus' Prayer of Unity

It also seems that another dimension is touched by the Sister who is able to express another culture than what seems to be called "American." By the way, as another diversion, we have come to claim exclusive use of the name "American" and every other country on the continent has to name itself in relation to us (United States). Are not Canadians and Mexicans, Americans? To return to the point, persons who contain within themselves the flower or fruit of the education, social, religious development of a race hold us accountable to the roots of our particular history. Many persons would assert that they would be curious to know their family tree. A person who facilitates the remembrance of the past in all the good senses makes an invaluable contribution to the present. All that was good lives on and is given enough life to enable the community to grow in wisdom.

Another aspect of a culturally advantaged Sister is that very rarely there is the possibility of human ties outside of our "nationalism" that can admit new channels of truth to the community. The truth is hard to come by today if we base our sources only in newspapers, radio and television. There is nothing more divisive and hampering to world peace than wrong information or ignorance. Myths that are built up are usually justification for my non-involvement. This is a reality that women in Religious life have experienced on a personal level. We have been guilty of much destruction by "labeling," etc.

Should Minorities Continue to Wait for the Welcome?

For me a culturally advantaged Sister brings richness, opens the community to others and their needs, has a contribution to make toward making the Church truly catholic or universal. We realize the developing trend toward pluralism as our society tries to reconcile the sins it has been guilty of by racism and prejudice. If we are to be holy we must really love all persons. How can a group of people believe we really love and believe in them when we reject their daughters who ask to join our congregation?

If we cannot learn to live in unity in a Religious community with Sisters of diverse races and perhaps even some creeds, how can I or anyone hope for world unity? No one who is not really considered equal to me will be able to form a unity. It is a necessary condition for being truly united and our Father God realized this when he sent his son so that we might be united to him.

There is perhaps more we could say on some of the deeper implications that culture has on spirituality and the apostolate but this would involve a whole other dissertation. The seeds of these implications are, however, contained in the previous thoughts. We strive to make real for the world the prayer of Jesus, "That all may be one as you Father in me and I in thee."

Some Suggestions for Community Reflections on:

The Culturally Advantaged Sister:
Implications for Total Community Formation

- What message has been communicated to your community in its re-flections on the presence or absence of members from different racial groups?
- Who has taken leadership in your community on racial issues? What subtle racial prejudices might be operating in your community regard-ing: vocation and formation policies, choice of ministry and lifestyle, education, and opportunities for leadership?
- Sister Maria presented a challenge for the future in speaking of the need for Religious to live in communities of diverse races as a sign that the Church is universal and can therefore be a sign of hope for world unity. Can you suggest ways to bring this about more quickly?
- Many, especially Religious Brothers, are telling us that this is the time of "brotherhood and sisterhood." How can Religious better com-municate to each other the experience of being known and loved as sisters and brothers?

A Dialogue on Learning Communities

In the past, historians, writers, and Religious spoke of Religious life as a school — a school of love, a school of conversion, a school of prayer. Today educators speak of living/learning centers, and we refer to Religious communities as learning communities. There is need, then, for educators, futurists, and Religious to come together to create models for future learning — models that are humane, imaginative, and innovative.

In her paper, Sister Alice St. Hilaire traces the history and evolution of the Sister Formation movement and challenges formation personnel to carry forward the pioneering spirit of the movement. After summarizing developments in the field of continuing education, Sister Marlene Halpin suggests ways that formation personnel can use the principles of androgogy in planning their programs. In the final article, Sister Mary Ann Barnhorn describes three intercommunity formation programs that have resulted from cooperative planning.

21

Sister Formation: A Decade Later

Alice St. Hilaire, SP

In the early 1950s, we who are now the middle generation were relatively new members of our communities when Pope Pius XII called every Sister to be all she could be and to be totally available to the Church and its mission. Every Sister was to be prepared as well as, if not better than, her lay counterpart for whatever her work might be.

With the energy and vision of their predecessors, American Sisters set about to discover what might be necessary to translate the Pope's call into reality. Led by Sister Mary Emil, IHM, a woman with a special charism, the early pioneers mobilized through the NCEA, gathered data throughout Europe and the United States, obtained a Ford Grant and spent the summer of 1956 writing the Everett Curriculum.° They negotiated with bishops, pastors, universities, educators, and their own communities — Sister Formation was in motion.

I will attempt, first, to articulate in summary form the main thrust of the Sister Formation Movement. Second, I will look at some of the key differences between Sister Formation in the '50s and '60s and finally, I will make some observations about the impact of all of this on the present and the future. I am especially concerned about the continuity of some essential and viable in-

° *Report of Everett Curriculum Workshop*, sponsored by the Sister Formation Conference of the National Catholic Educational Association (Heiden's Mailing Bureau, Seattle, Washington, September, 1956). Page references are to this report.

tents of Sister Formation, which must have their expression today in other forms or structures.

Philosophy of the Movement

For the creators of Sister Formation, awareness of new horizons and of the need for every Sister to live and work out of a world-consciousness, demanded emphasis on education. The content and quality of that education should be dictated by the Sister's role in the fast-changing global society. Education of the Sister was seen to have "a complex, though unified, objective" (p. 18), with emphasis on two facets — the intellectual and the spiritual.

"A new term, Sister Formation . . . includes Religious formation, intellectual formation, and a planned integration of the two. The end which Religious communities set out to achieve as a result of this total formation program is a Sister in whom maturity, balance, culture, and competency are united with spiritual fruitfulness to produce a saintly and therefore effective Religious — effective both personally and socially" (p. 18).

A carefully planned configuration of courses was begun with a philosophical and psychological study of the human person, which progressed through a full theological development, in world, Church, American and 20th century history, a sequence in the social sciences of sociology, economics, political science, and geography, and finished with two integrating courses, national and international issues, taught from an interdisciplinary approach. This core was designed for 1) an in-depth grasp of social reality as formed of and formed by human persons, 2) an understanding of the basic principles of each of the social science disciplines, 3) a comprehension of the demands of the common good, 4) the forming of responsible personal political convictions, and 5) intelligent interpretation of ecclesial documents dealing with social questions (pp. 61-62). This core was rounded out by the balance of the courses normally included in a liberal arts program, and a high quality, well planned, co-curricular program designed to "complement and supplement the credit courses of the undergraduate pre-service curriculum" (p. 119). Professional preparation that followed was built on this foundation.

Effects of Early Efforts at Sister Formation

For the sake of brevity, I will state the most significant effects/values contributions of this period as I see them.

True education liberates. The vision and action of the leaders in the Sister Formation movement itself were evidence of the stirring of the Spirit that was fast leading to Vatican II. Although not the sole agent, Sister Formation was a primary contributor to the visibility and growing influence of women in leadership roles in the Church and society today. The mystique of the hidden life has given way to a climate in which personal responsibility, confronting of options, and outspoken convictions are the norm.

Cooperation among Religious communities. This cooperation brought the Sister to a new level of truth about who she is, and what it is to be with other Christians a member of the one body. Happily, those participating in joint formation programs formed lasting friendships with Sisters of various communities, and their experience from the beginning was that of unity enriched by diversity.

Informed Sisters. A basic of the Sister Formation rationale was that to be an effective servant of the people of God, a Sister must be informed. She needed to know the reality of God as the ultimate meaning of persons and the reality of the world as it exists. This knowledge had to be not only a "common sense" knowledge and the personal experience that is essential, but also an educated perception that checks the "common sense" tendency to oversimplify and personalize social issues.

Pioneering Spirit. One of the most important aspects of the entire movement was the pioneering spirit that is true to founders of Religious communities, to the gospel, and to the reality of the pilgrim Church. One has only to look as far back as the initiators and implementers of Sister Formation for inspiring examples of boldness, endurance, and readiness to risk.

Clearly, Sister Formation carries its share of responsibility for the dramatic, and sometimes traumatic, changes of recent years in Religious communities and in the Church. Occasionally someone points a knowing finger and says, "I told you it wouldn't work." Another expresses regret at the great waste of talent, time, personnel and financial outlay for an effort that seemingly lasted such a short time, wondering why it failed. The truth is Religious communities could never have come from where they were in 1956 to where they now are without the whole of Sister Formation, or something equally bold, visionary, and full of risk.

There are a number of good reasons why the Sister Formation format of a decade ago is not being restored today. None of these reasons spells failure. All of them speak of growth. Formation for tomorrow must not be repetitive: but it must be inspired by and continuous with what was yesterday and is today.

Key Differences Between Sister Formation Yesterday and Today

Sister Formation is different today. The differences in formation are necessarily reflective of the changes that have occurred in Religious communities. They reflect the impact of future shock in the Church and in society. The contemporary world view has become process vs. essential. The dignity and rights of the person are regarded at once as the most important and the most ignored of all realities. In the Church and in Religious communities, plurality has replaced the previous uniformity; collegiality is a byword; social justice and quality are gospel concepts seeping anew into our consciousness. Communities have undergone radical changes in lifestyles, in apostolic involvements, in governmental structures, and in greatly increased individual response and responsibility.

Formation today differs from that of the past in that although there are fewer vocations, those who do enter possess a greater degree of education and experience, in addition to a developed life of prayer. Formation usually takes place either in small houses, which may or may not be established primarily for formation purposes, or as an adjunct to a mother house or other institution. The interpretation of canonical separation of novices is greatly modified. Most communities have some type of formation team. Formation programs, as such, seem to vary from the indefinite, to whatever develops year by year, to a reasonably well-defined set of goals and procedures. Whatever the stage of development, formation is more concerned with the person and the developmental process than with a curriculum such as the Everett Curriculum.

If we allow that the ideals and effects of the Sister Formation movement of a decade ago may be summed up in 1) liberation of the person, 2) increased realization of oneness in the Body of Christ, 3) Sisters informed for effective ministry, and 4) the pioneer spirit of risking all for the sake of the kingdom, then we can agree that it is in this spirit that we must move forward.

Liberation of the person. In the original Sister Formation plan, a liberal arts education was considered basic. That should continue to be considered basic today and a regular part of the formation process if an incoming member does not have it. In addition, every structure, every decision, every personal encounter, must be aimed at realizing not a program, but a person. There are some practical ways of making that happen:

If the entire formation team shares responsibility for the whole program, and if it numbers enough persons for the beginner to have a real choice of a personal formation director, then a person in formation may choose to continue with the same director through all the stages of formation. This assures both rapport between the Sister in formation and her director, and continuity for the individual, in addition to deepening integration at several levels.

If formation communities include not only team members and new members, but also others involved in full-time apostolates, the situation will tend to be more real and less contrived with all members of the house on an equal footing. Those in formation will be our best teachers in this respect.

If the formation team functions as a team of *co*-directors rather than as a director with assistants, the Sisters in formation will have a model of relationships among persons with distinct roles, functioning as equals. If the formation team values openness, participation, and respect for the person, it will see that the Sister in formation is responsibly involved in all planning and decisions affecting her life.

If we are wise we will also maximize time flexibility at all stages of formation according to individual need (e.g., interruption of the canonical year, three to nine years of temporary commitment, etc.). These features contribute to the realization that the individual's good and the community's good are in concert, and that discernment of one's vocation in freedom and truth can be pursued free from the pressures of a group or concepts of success/failure. If our formation process is truly liberating, a decision not to enter a community or not to make a final commitment will be as profoundly a decision for God as is a decision to respond to him within community.

All of this "personalization" must be viewed in the context of an intimate and growing relationship with God, nourished and guided by solid theology and wise direction.

Realization of oneness in the body of Christ. Sister Formation of a decade ago provided significant avenues for the realization of our unity in Christ in many intercommunity efforts, as well as in the intensive and extensive education in the social sciences proposed in the Everett Curriculum. Writers of the curriculum recognized that experience in apostolic endeavors was also an essential ingredient for this realization. However, in most instances the length and intensity of the education process left little energy or time for more than a token involvement. It is important that the formation process today include meaningful apostolic involvement according to the person's readiness.

Another aspect of this unity will be realized if the new members of a community see and experience their Religious community as a body of women who see Christ in and are Christ to one another. This enables them to meet and be Christ in every other meeting and event. They will deepen this sense of oneness as they further experience being missioned by their community to their apostolic activities.

Unity will be experienced in a vital way if incoming members from the beginning are included as an integral part of the larger Religious family through participation in community assemblies, meetings, and celebrations. It will be deepened if they find their community involved at various levels of cooperative effort with our Religious and civic agents to bring healing, justice, and truth to others.

Sisters informed for effective ministry. This ideal was perhaps one of the best realized in the Sister Formation movement. The main thrust of the curriculum was directed toward a solid intellectual grasp of the many-faceted complexion of the human person and society as the base for effecting radical social change according to the gospel message. Today, the awareness of the need for social change and active concern for the oppressed is a growing reality, but activity is frequently entered into with relatively little comprehension of the underlying theological and sociological principles. Because we do not now have Sister Formation Colleges, and because many come to us already professionally prepared, careful planning for in-depth understandings is essential if Sisters are to be effective precisely as Religious women of the Church.

The pioneer spirit of risk. The founders of Sister Formation took the risk of creating and implementing a program that interrupted whole systems of operation and whole patterns of thought — not only as it concerned formation itself, but as it affected the entire Religious community, relations with pastors and bishops, staffing of institutions, and almost every facet of their existence.

The readiness to risk as much must continue to characterize Religious communities today and in the future. In formation, specifically, it seems that communities must commit personnel for even a few persons in formation, and regard formation as an on-going creative process consistent with a dynamic concept of reality. A good formation team should have in its membership a rich variety of personalities with wisdom and expertise, and with an active and growing spiritual life. They should have a basic agreement on their philosophies of person, of Religious life, and of formation, solid commitment to the work of formation, a genuine respect for every other team member, and an ability to work well together. Among themselves and in cooperation with the larger community, they need to have the genius and the creativity to combine guidelines that provide basic stability and clarity with operational practices that meet the individual where she is and assist her forward.

Conclusion: Same Spirit, but a Different Emphasis

I have characterized the original Sister Formation program as valuing and effecting 1) liberation of the person, 2) increased realization of oneness in the Body of Christ, 3) Sisters informed for effective ministry, and 4) the spirit of risk. I have proposed that these same values need to characterize the spirit of Sister Formation today and as it moves into the future.

In highlighting the differences between the initial Sister Formation movement and Sister Formation in its present complexion, it seems that these differences might be summed up in a single difference of emphasis. Sister Formation a decade ago sought as its objective "a Sister in whom maturity, balance, culture, and competency are united with spiritual fruitfulness to produce a saintly and therefore effective Religious" (p. 18), primarily through an education model. The curriculum became the core and the integrating factor of all the facets of the formation program. Sister Formation today seeks the same goals, but with less concern for curriculum. The emphasis is rather on the person and the development process. This is an evolution within a much larger evolution, and Sisters could hardly be faithful to their own mandate to timeliness and effectiveness if this evolution were not in process.

Yet, as in all evolutionary processes, the movement forward will be most truly responsive to the Spirit if those involved build on the wisdom and achievements of those who preceded them. In their new emphasis on person and development, Religious communities must not neglect the formative power of a solid base in the arts and sciences and in-depth study in some given area. They must also be aware that the transition of viewing and experiencing reality as process rather than as essence in no way eliminates the necessity of continuing study, planning and evaluation, both for overall formation goals and policies, and for each individual in the formation process.

Adequate education and clearly defined goals for formation are values easily lost in the particular evolution that Religious communities are experiencing today. If they ignore them, the emphasis on person will almost surely become a tyranny, with Religious experiencing reverting to a romantic, introverted piety, with apostolic efforts having no more lasting effect than those of the proverbial do-gooder. If they preserve them and integrate them into enlightened, spirited, always developing formation processes centered in the person, especially the person of Christ, they can rightly hope that progression into the future will be a continuing fulfillment of Pope Pius' call to total availability to Church and its mission.

Some Suggestions for Community Reflection on:

Sister Formation: A Decade Later

- The founders of Sister Formation risked much in "creating and implementing a program that interrupted whole systems of operation and whole patterns of thought — not only as it concerned formation itself, but as it affected the entire Religious community — relations with pastors and bishops, staffing of institutions, and almost every facet of their existence." What risks are necessary now to bring about the liberation of persons and structures?

- What is the responsibility of a new member in your community to plan and implement a solid formation program? What responsibility do formation personnel bear in planning and implementing formation programs?

- Is it any longer important for Religious to be in touch with the charism, history, and evolution of the Sister Formation Movement in the United States, or have other organizations sufficiently taken up the challenge to develop women Religious?

- The Leadership Board of the Sister Formation Conference held its fall board meeting in 1975 on the weekend after the Futureshop on Formation. The board voted at this meeting to open full membership in the Conference to non-canonical communities and to men Religious. It also voted to change the name of the conference either to the National Religious Formation Conference or to the National Ministerial Formation Conference. What in your opinion will be the effects of these changes? What other changes might you suggest?

22

Continuing Education: Attitudes and Reality

Marlene Halpin, OP

Perhaps one of the more difficult problems faced by young Sisters is dealing with the chasm between their fine formation programs and the convent/ministry situations encountered in their first assignment.

Perhaps one of the more difficult questions formation directors face is: "How good a formation program ought we offer to young people?" When they are exposed to good, divergent theological thinking; when they learn to create satisfying liturgical experiences; when they are expected to (and do) work collegially; when they have learned to be open, accepting, flexible; what happens to them when they reenter the real world? Often disillusionment and frustration; sometimes trauma and catastrophe.

What might we do for changing and changeable young people when we can anticipate their having to live and work with unchanging (and seeing-no-need-to-change) others? I propose a consideration of continuing education with three levels of application: for people in formation; for formation personnel; for the people in ministry.

Continuing Education

Androgogy (the art and science of helping adults learn) is different from pedagogy. Adult learning is more independent, self-initiated, stems from experienced personal or professional needs, and is intended for immediate use. However, androgogy still needs a great deal of development.

That human persons evidence an innate desire to learn is a commonplace of everyday existence. People like to know. People like to do what they do with competence. That life-long education is a desirable component in a contemporary person's attempt to deal with his/her various roles and role expectations satisfactorily, is also becoming more evident. Allen Tough's 1971 studies show that adults engage in an average of eight self-initiated projects a year, using about 700 hours.[1]

Forty-five years ago Alfred North Whitehead noted that — for the first time in human history — significant cultural changes occur during a normal life span. Implications for education are radical. People need to be prepared to recognize, plan, use, live with processes of continuing change. Strong shifts in understanding the nature and purpose of education as well as the role of the teacher are taking place.

If human beings are viewed as empty pages to be written on, as requiring external forces to produce action, then the purpose of education can be seen as the transmission of knowledge and culture, and the role of the teacher is to be the transmitter of information. Teachers teach. Maybe students learn.

If human beings are viewed as growing from an internal life source, capable of progressive development followed by self and social improvement, then the purpose of education is each person's growth in the fullness of his/her unique expression of personhood, and the role of the teacher is to facilitate these on-going processes.

Reality and Attitudes

Because I subscribe to the second of these options, I suggest that attitudinal approaches to several current realities be examined:

• The reality that, for many among us, imparting "good, solid material" is the task of education. Sensitivities, skills, beliefs, feelings belong to an unidentified somewhere else, but not in education.

• The reality that, still for many among us, it is understood that when "schooling" is finished, "education" is finished. ("I'll never take another examination again," vows the degree recipient.)

• The reality that, while some would like further education, lack of time and money are all but insurmountable obstacles.

• The reality that, while some would think about "taking something," they wonder if it's worth it: especially when peer support and accountability are lacking and no recognition given.

• Then there is a larger reality. The rate of change, rapidity of communication, mobility of persons, fluidity of roles and role expectations in one person's lifetime demand that education make provision for skills (relational and career) development, value consciousness, and attitude formation.

In the light of human nature (which naturally wants to know and naturally delights in competency) and the condition of our world, many people's attitudes toward continuing education could be enlarged enjoyably. We all have numerous roles: our own self-identity; ourselves as family/community members; as friend/neighbor/citizen; as worker/learner/consumer; as Religious/social/leisured person. Fulfilling these roles — individually or in any given combination — requires a multiplicity of skills. Acquiring and sharpening them is the work of life-long education.

I would like to propose the following assumptions:
1) human beings grow from within;
2) people are capable of responsible and enjoyable self-direction;
3) internalized learning is effective learning;
4) education is a life-long process of acquiring and improving knowledge, understanding, skills, sensitivities, attitudes, interests, values;
5) effective education calls for facilitators and resources;

I then propose Rouch's definition of continuing education:

Continuing Education is an individual's personally designed learning program which begins when basic formal education ends, and continues throughout a career and beyond. An unfolding process, it links together personal study and reflection and participation in organized group events.[2]

If his definition and the prior assumptions are acceptable, then I can propose a series of problems for work on continuing education in Sister formation.

Life-long Education

We must recognize the *reality* of the *need* for life-long education and the *attitude* toward that: both among Sisters and those with whom they will work.

As I view this problem, it seems to me that a little common-sense reflection identifies the need. Attitudes toward it frequently are negative. Part of this is caused by the identification of education with schooling, and schooling with imposed didactic input and inadequate, frustrating testing. The legacy of these things renders many not-young people resistant to continuing education. (They've had enough of *that*, thank you.) Sometimes they are adverse to staff members participating in it. Time and money are not allocated.

Problems: 1) How, if you are convinced of the need for life-long education, can you be an effective change agent in your situation? 2) How do you educate people in formation: a) to have an habitually inquiring mind, b) to be appropriate change agents in their real world of ministry?

Different Methods

There is a need for different teaching methods for adults. The educational scene today is quite uneven. Individual and programmed instruction, external degree programs, nontraditional studies, ministry degrees, use of groups, do happen. But not universally. And not necessarily well.

Problem: How to awaken in teachers a desire to master skills involved in inquiry learning, and provide opportunities for this to happen? In an immediate sense, how will formation personnel become proficient in fostering productive thinking skills in their young people, in helping them master the skills of self-directed learning?[3]

Motivation

Motivation — in spite of the fact that we naturally desire to learn and to do well — remains the single, greatest pragmatic problem facing continuing education in ministry. Most other professionals often have more tangible rewards: promotions, pay increases, fulfilling criteria for re-licensing.

In ministry we have genuine problems in motivation. Where there is low self-concept, self-initiated projects are unexpected. Eugene Kennedy's study of American priests shows underdevelopment in such areas as: human relations, using the priestly/Religious role "authority" as a substitute for competency, in psycho-sexual identity (which can precipitate many "Father-Sister" problems), in attitudes toward authority.

Problems: 1) How do you — formation personnel — help your young people achieve a healthy, realistic self-image? 2) How do you prepare your young people to deal with underdeveloped colleagues/Superiors? With sometimes irrational authority? How do you help educate them to be effective change agents, even from the beginning of their ministry?

As far as I know, there are no magic, cure-all answers. But there are some general guidelines and some attempts being made to deal with these challenges.

Recommendations

Awareness of the human need for interdependence in personal and work situations, support from and accountability to peer group and superiors, allocation of time and funds for counselling and educational experiences are seen as essential to life-long education. Whether or not we in Church service favor being called "professionals," it seems obvious to me that we cannot be at once responsible servants and incompetent ministers.

Let me conclude with these recommendations and the hope for some vibrant discussion:

1) formation personnel: examine and formulate your own knowledge of and attitudes toward life-long education;

2) follow this with appropriate personal planning;

3) have your young people do likewise;

4) prepare them for Religious life, by all means: but include in their education the ability to be change agents.

All of this, I submit, makes for happier, more realistic living: as women Religious, as persons engaged in active ministry. It will also keep life interesting for us and for all who encounter us.

References

1.   Allen Tough. *The Adult's Learning Projects*. Institute for Studies in Education, Toronto, 1971. Cf. also John and Lela Hendrix. *Experiential Education*. Abingdon Press, New York, 1975; and Cyril O. House. *The Design of Education*. Jossey-Bass, San Francisco, 1973.

2.   Mark A. Rouch. *Competent Ministry: A Guide to Effective Continuing Education*. Abingdon Press, New York, 1974, pp. 16-17. Cf. his "Motivation for Continuing Education: Some Preliminary Considerations." Paper for *Sachem*, June, 1975.

3.   Malcolm Knowles. *The Adult Learner: A Neglected Species*. Gulf Publishing Co., Houston, 1973, pp. 160-164, and "Issues in Adult Learning Psychology," *Adult Leadership*. March, 1974. pp. 300-316. Cf. also Gerald J. Pine and Peter J. Horne. "Principles and Conditions for Learning in Adult Education," *Adult Leadership*. October, 1969. pp. 108-110; 126-134.

Some Suggestions for Community Reflection on:

Continuing Education: Attitudes and Reality

- Formulate and share in succession:
    a) a personal
    b) a local community
    c) a total community-wide
  statement "of knowledge of and attitudes toward life-long education."
- Create and share:
    a) your personal
    b) your local community
    c) your total community
  plan for continuing education of members.
- Discuss the three needs and the problems suggested by Sister Marlene in her article.
- After finding out what other Religious communities are doing to deal with the problems listed below, sit down as a group and strategize to see how your community could better deal with the problems of:
    1) satisfying ministries for each Religious
    2) support systems
    3) accountability
    4) rewards and recognition

23

Intercommunity Formation Programs:
The Cincinnati Experience

Mary Ann Barnhorn, SNDdeN

Parishes, dioceses, local and national movements call upon us as
Sisters to utilize our experience in community renewal when we
participate in the effort to build parishes and dioceses that incorporate the vision of community called for in *Lumen Gentium*,
and the sense of mission described in *Gaudium et Spes*, the *Constitution on the Church in the Changing World*. The renewal of
our own internal structures was a beginning, an apprenticeship if
you will, in a process that holds within it the potential of changing
a parish, a diocese, and a Church. The process involved evolving
from a group of persons who do what they are told to do, to a
community of believers who respond to the gospel mandate to
build the kingdom. This kingdom is that ever-expanding community of believers who recognize that God is their Father and who
meet Christ in one another as they grow in freedom to die and rise
within him each day. It is, as Richard McBrien so aptly says, "a
matter of the world becoming human."

A Broader and Deeper Vision Informs New Programs

In order to take our rightful place in the building of the kingdom,
Sisters must expand their vision of the mission of Jesus. It is this
vision of the mission of Jesus which must be the umbrella under

which we plan and develop programs in both initial and on-going formation.

Four years ago, the novice directors in the Cincinnati, Ohio area began to meet once a month to explore the possibilities of collaboration. Our concern at that time was to provide quality input for new members of our communities. We each had one or two novices, and expediency brought us together. It is significant for me, however, that it is much more than expediency that keeps us together. A vital factor in the development of the three programs worked out to date has been the vision of Cincinnati's then associate vicar of Religious, Sister Elizabeth Cashman, SC.

As we continued our monthly meetings, the question that surfaced was: Do we want to come together one day a week to hear several lectures, or do we want to develop a program that will provide an integrated experience in communal living, liturgical prayer, and theological input? We opted for the latter. The intercommunity novitiate program that has developed approaches the themes of covenant, Jesus Christ, Church, and mission from the aspect of the human, the scriptural and the theological. The year is divided into phases, and each phase focuses upon one of these themes. We do not try to duplicate what is already available in universities; our aim is to provide a total experience which will enable each novice to deepen her understanding of the meaning of Religious life in our time. A vital part of this Studies in Spirituality Program is the in-service opportunities provided for formation directors. Currently nine different Orders from a tri-state area participate in Studies in Spirituality, which began its third year in the fall of 1975.

Intercommunity Program of Preparation
for Final Commitment

The second intercommunity program which we have developed in Cincinnati is a summer program for Sisters preparing for final commitment. In this program we focus on the biblical themes related to commitment and Religious life. There is a time each day for reflection, Eucharistic celebration, and theological input.

Both Sister Elizabeth Cashman and I were convinced that ongoing formation must be a priority for Religious women. In 1974 we began to work on a program which we have called an Active

Spirituality for a Global Community. This year-long, live-in program is predicated on the belief that the monastic formation which we had as young Sisters did not address itself to the asceticism of leadership nor to the social issues of our day. This new program is a response to the recent teachings of the Church, best summed up in the oft-quoted sentence: "Action on behalf of justice is constitutive of the gospel message."

It seems to me that although we often speak of active spirituality, there has been little attempt to articulate the source and the context of such a spirituality. The program, An Active Spirituality for the Global Community, attempts to provide an opportunity for each participant to arrive at her own awareness of the meaning of active spirituality in her life as a Religious woman. The model upon which the program is built is reflection/action/reflection.

The first phase of the program is spent in Cincinnati and includes the scriptural themes of discipleship, kingdom, justice, sin, city, sacramental theology, psychology of leadership, political theology, theology of liberation, and seminars on global issues. The second phase is spent in Washington, D.C. where Father Bryan Hehir of the USCC, Sister Carol Coston of Network and Mr. Joseph Holland of the Center of Concern will facilitate the group's addressing itself to the phenomenon of power and powerlessness in the global community.

In January the group returns to Cincinnati for Attitudes in Human Encounter, and Moral-Theological Anthropology. The entire month of February is to be spent in San Antonio at the Mexican American Cultural Center (MACC). MACC was chosen because the staff at the center is able to expose oppression and injustice and also to reflect on the causes of oppression and the call to systemic change. In March, April and May, Christological themes, incarnational spirituality, and the theology of apostolic Religious life are presented in the service of synthesis.

It is my conviction that such intercommunity programs as we have developed are not merely a matter of expediency; they witness to the collaboration and the expanding sense of community in the Church. In all of these programs planned for active women Religious the unifying factor is the mission of the Church.

It is this mission of Jesus, extended and specified by the Church, that is the focal point of active spirituality.

Some Suggestions for Community Reflection on:

Intercommunity Formation Programs: The Cincinnati Experience

- Is it wise to support formation programs which are not cooperative or intercommunity in nature and sponsorship?
- List and evaluate the efforts your community has made to further cooperative planning and programming among Religious, in your diocese and in your geographic area.
- Brainstorm with an ecumenical group on the possible effects of creating a new formation model: a diocesan or regional Ministerial Learning Center open to all persons who wish preparation for ministry.

A Dialogue on Projected Tomorrows

In the first article, Sister Shawn Madigan challenges formation personnel to be futurists and corporate planners. She describes the need to move from a European to an American model of formation and from a 20th century to a 21st century model. Sister Louise Dempsey defines "feminists" and shows how feminism is the path to full humanization. She makes suggestions about the role of prophets and women leaders in the Church. Sister Nancy Swift is convinced that if we are to move beyond the present stage of renewal, both liturgists and formation personnel must begin to focus on the non-verbal, symbolic aspects of liturgy. She stresses the need to value the feminine mode of being and way of knowing. In the final paper, Sister Rhonda Meister, as a young Religious, asks difficult questions of formation personnel regarding their own obedience to the Church's call to justice.

24

Projected Tomorrows and Effects on Formation Today

Shawn Madigan, CSJ

As soon as Jesus invited the disciples to be in the world but not of the world and to love one another as he first loved, he gave both direction and ambiguity to future centuries of Religious life. The Church — in its broadest meaning — would constantly require renewal in the spirit of Jesus in order to assess whether it was in the world in his name or of the world in its own name. In addition, it would constantly have to examine its laws to see if they were enabling believers to love the Lord more deeply, or if they were prejudging believers to be unloving and so restricting measurement of love to external practices only. As the post-Vatican Church continues the constant call to renewal in the Spirit it invites Religious communities to look with it at the quality of discipleship professedly theirs.

To do this in a realistic way requires a context of Christian history, for Christian history is not only a past and present phenomenon; it is a future promise as well. One cannot be effective in today's world, attempting to understand it and give it meaningful direction, unless that triple facet of history — past, present, future — is consciously realized. The society in which we live is very future conscious, and that future thrust has found its way in varying degrees into both the content and structure of Religious life, as might well be expected. Changes in value emphasis as forecast for the '80s and predicted trends are already happening in Religious life and in society and these will continue to happen, gaining momentum if we choose to have them do so.

Shifts of Emphasis of Value Trends

Some of these value trends will be synthesized and summarized here with more extensive futuristic reading available in the cited articles in the references. I will list the value forecasting trends, but apply only one of them here to formation, so that you can get an idea of how future trends can be used in assessment of community direction, formation programs, and so on. Just in case the trends seem to pose for you a rather disheartening challenge to creativity, let me add that all of society faces the enormous task of adapting and restructuring both private and public value systems. As values emphasis shifts, there can be expected increase in conflict and confrontation, for that is normative. There will be an increased "groaning" of America before the "greening" can happen and we should expect it as people who are in the world. The advantage for Christians is that the waiting period of conflict and groaning can be a hopeful awareness of that need for the final revelation of the kingdom never here fully.

These are the basic shifts in emphasis of predicted value trends:

- There will be increasing stress on the qualitative (better) rather than the quantitative (more) aspects of life.
- A growing movement toward deeper interdependence — particularly among the better educated — will replace excessive independence or dependence attitudes of adults.
- Primary concern about private need fulfillment will give way to concern for more public needs.
- Personal self-development and aspirations of members of an organization will take gradual priority over organizational convenience, order, efficiency, and expenditures for profit.
- Increased demand for participation will continue to replace the old authoritarian or executive power.
- Growth in anti-authoritarianism will continue to result in greater alienation from outmoded institutions, and there will be a reduction of personal toleration for any form of self-alienation.
- Diversity and pluralism will continue to replace uniformity and centralization.

- The leisure ethic will receive as much emphasis as the work ethic, with the trend toward a three-day week increasing until 1980.
- The consciousness of growing intimacy needs may see a new flourishing of family life and community life as essential life supports in an ambiguous society. This will replace the prior career satisfaction support that was characteristic of many people in the past and present era of history.
- Promotion of and increased acceptance of change is already replacing the former preservation of the status quo for organizational systems.

The Future is a Formation Concern

All institutions that wish to avoid a collision course for the future will need a built-in capability for rapid adjustment to new roles and tasks in order to keep pace with the changing needs of society. Any institution that cannot adapt quickly is destined to become increasingly more outmoded, non-credible, and self-destructive. Though that is properly a concern for the whole Church, as well as the total Religious community, it is especially a formation concern — for it is that program which must be preparatory for the future, enabling individuals to live meaningfully and flexibly in the pace of change demanded by the twenty-first century. Whatever form that program takes, it can expect to meet with some suspicion and misunderstanding from those who still live in the nineteenth and twentieth centuries.

What are some implications of Trend One for formation personnel? The trend states that there will be increasing emphasis on qualitative rather than quantitative assessment of values, life and so on. You may recall that the American Dream was based on quantitative values. The more money you have, the more friends you have, the more cars you have, the bigger the house you have, the more material everything you have, etc., the happier you will be. The Church was no stranger to quantitative assessment either. The more Masses you attend, the more indulgences you gain, the more communions a parish distributed, the more children married couples had, the more money in the collection box, the bigger the church and school, the more extensive and important the diocese over which you were bishop, the more priests and Sisters, etc., the better and happier the Church. Though there are grains of truth in such assessments, there were also grains of untruth.

Let us look at one question asked of Religious communities. How many people are coming to join you? That is a quantitative question, the assumption being that the more you get, the more vital your community must be. But according to future assessment, that is the wrong question. The question should be — if Trend One is right — "What kind of people are joining you?" Are they persons seeking security because they are afraid of — or reject — the world? Or are they basically secure persons who love the world as Christ loved it, and are willing and capable of living with that insecurity demanded of all Christians who seek the Lord in order to bring and find him in the world?

A study done by Cynthia Wedel (published in *Theology Today*, April, 1973) has some bearing on the above question. Her study concerned the issue of growing numbers of people in conservative churches and decreasing numbers in more liberal churches. Her conclusion was that liberal churches had the major problem of a false presumption that Christians really knew the basics of faith from the accidentals; thus building a deeper faith was built on liberation that did not really exist, whereas the conservative churches continued to stress dogmatic certainties and quantitative practices as assurances of faith which gave people very definite criteria for measurement of goodness.

The ultimate question is, of course, whether the criteria have so increased that the Lord has decreased as the measure of holiness. I raise this point not to evaluate decline in church attendance, but merely to point out that any organization, church, community that stresses qualitative assessment and thus a deep quality of commitment — whether that be Religious life, marriage, or single life — can expect to have fewer and fewer persons able to live at such a level of qualitative existence. That is not a judgment on society today; I believe it is merely a new awakening of what the mustard seed parable is all about. That parable is difficult for a quantitative society — as we ourselves have grown accustomed to — to really understand.

Models of Formation: A Viable One for Tomorrow

There is another question flowing from the qualitative trend, and one which formation personnel have been asked to consider since

Vatican II. What model or program is most viable for formation today? There are two basic models: a more quantitative replicative model and a qualitative mutual growth model. The difference in models has been an object of educational consideration as well as Church consideration. As these models can be applied to formation, the characteristics would be as follows:

The quantitative replicative model influences others to take on the form or external actions of the initiator, and thus the novice director must be exemplary in the forms of the institute. The model involves a certain separation mentality: separation from parents, friends, from a variety of age groupings, secular studies, service involvement. This is all in an attempt to find the Lord in a specialized setting of organized prayer and assurance of prayer times, religious studies rather than secular ones, spiritual direction, perhaps minimal apostolic involvement and relatively little ambiguity, as the situation is quite controlled. That model was effective — and could still be effective — as long as the other Religious homes are only slight variations from the model. It is easy to teach of Religious life in that quantitative replicative model, because the external measurable aspects are quite clearly visible.

The quantity of time available for prayer and reflection are indicators of the value placed on each: external objects of vows make it easy to check on fidelity to vocation; criteria for acceptable membership are quite clear because they are externally tangible. Uniformity or centralization assure a secure degree of similar activity. A certain amount of dependence is presumed in that model rather than creative attempts to be responsible for one's life; that was a good model when society operated in a similar pattern.

But today there is emerging another model that indicates a societal shift of emphasis from a quantitative to a qualitative mutual growth model. In this model, the form arises from the internal growth needs of the individual person. The spirit of the community is somehow lived and caught before it is formally reflected upon and thus taught. The spirituality of apostolic communities is finding the separation model quite contrary to the spirit of being in and for the world. Tensions of over-extension versus the time necessary for community to happen cannot be realistically

faced in a separation novitiate. Novitiate houses placed in moth-
erhouse contexts make them unlike other community houses,
adding to the adjustment later. External measurable aspects of
membership requirements and vows give way in this model to the
demands of spiritual-psychological membership, which is a
deeper qualitative issue and thus more difficult to explain and
assess. The essential measurement for how faithfully the vows are
being lived is no longer only external practice, but rather relationship to each other, to the community as a whole, to the
Church, to the world — but most essentially to Jesus Christ.

The former model of separation was based on the European
model of separation that began to change as soon as Religious set
foot in America, discovering that in this land only animals had
high walls or fences arbund them — but not people. American
values caused a gradual shift in models, for it was new wine slowly fermenting in old wineskins. Present models of formation acknowledge that such new wine indeed cannot be poured into old
wineskins without losing that wine or else breaking the wineskins,
depending on how one wishes to look at it.

Formation Personnel as Corporate Planners

At any rate, you are corporate planners for the future, whether
your community considers you as such or not. As planners, you
have responsibility for the future of Christ's kingdom in a special
way, and thus future trends must be part of on-going evaluation of
programs. Do the programs provide the experience that will be
similar to your particular community's spirituality as lived in local
communities? Does the program facilitate healthy personal adjustment to on-going change and ambiguity that demands confidence, interdependence, low defense mechanisms, creative responsibility in bringing about needed change so that total communities eventually will be creating the future instead of merely
responding to change inflicted by others? Do the programs encourage a basic honesty in searching together for the Lord in the
midst of business, tensions, noise, and every other aspect of the
worldliness that is one part of Christianity.

The future is only born out of the present moment of choice,
and that is the power which is yours in affecting those structures
that grow out of your community's experience of the Lord that

you invite others to recognize in themselves and reflect on. "The future is not really my responsibility," you may be thinking. But if that is what you are thinking, I would have to conclude by asking, "If not yours, then whose? And if change is not for now, then when?"

References

1. Gary Gappert. "Post Affluence: The Turbulent Transition to a Post-Industrial Society," *The Futurist*. Vol. III, No. 5, October, 1974, 212-216.

2. Clare W. Graves. "Human Nature Prepares for a Momentous Leap," *The Futurist*, Vol. VIII, No. 2, April, 1974, 72-89.

3. Barbara Hubbard. "Grow or Die: The Unifying Principle of Transformation," *The Futurist*, Vol. IX, No. 1, February, 1975, 15-17. This article is a review of George T. Lockland's book with the same title.

4. Cynthia Wedel. "Where the People Are," *Theology Today*, April 1973.

5. Ian Wilson. "The New Reformation: Changing Values and Institutional Goals," *The Futurist*, Vol. V, No. 3, June, 1971, 105-108.

Some suggestions for Community Reflection on:

Projected Tomorrows and Effects on Formation Today

- What professional preparation is provided for the present and future formation personnel in your community? How are formation personnel selected in your community?
- What is the best way for formation personnel to deal with the conflicts and confrontations that result from their efforts to prepare Sisters to minister in the 21st century?
- Exchange ideas on what changes are necessary in attitudes and structures so that formation can move from the quantitative model to the qualitative model of formation that Sister Shawn describes.
- Gather together a group of persons willing to brainstorm on the positive and negative consequences of the nine value-trends mentioned by Sister Shawn in her paper.

25

"Their Daughters Shall Prophesy..." Leadership for Women in Church and Society?

Louise Dempsey, CSJ

For too long in the Church the erroneous assumption has prevailed that leadership and women are incompatible entities. The Church for centuries has known a God whose identity is expressed in masculine terms. Even in the Church today ministry, decision-making, and service are viewed from the male standpoint, enveloped by their power and perpetuated by their control. Women's involvement in the patriarchical structure is unofficial, supportive, and impersonal. It is not so much that women are the objects of conscious violence as it is that they are ignored, not taken seriously, treated as nonpersons, or as ancillary agents to assist men who are the *norm* for persons in the Church.

But today a new type of person is emerging on the human scene and assuming a role of leadership not so prominent in the past. This person — woman as well as man — is increasingly conscious of personal worth and dignity. Vatican II's call to "respect the dignity of the human person"[1] is being taken seriously. Membership in an organization is not enough now; woman is demanding to be responsibly involved, to be a vital part of the forces that determine the *kind* of Church (or congregation) that it is to be and to become. The investment of one's very life in this membership gives priority to this attitude.

"Action on behalf of justice" is no mere cliché; it is required by the gospel and is "central to the Church's ministry."[2] Women must share the task of translating hierarchical pronouncements and Council directives into lived experiences for themselves and for those whom they serve. To be willing to share responsibly in such authority and leadership is a form of asceticism to which I believe each of us called. Superiors, men or women, cannot claim that it is their prerogative alone; it must be nurtured and exercised at all levels and stages.

Deprived of such leadership roles in the past, woman may find the call to this involvement more challenging because of contradictions she experiences. What we become grows out of what we have been, but the ecclesial role that woman has inherited is at variance with her own experience and understanding of herself. Prophets are needed to speak to the discrepancy. The need is to trust our own experience of God as real, and unique, and to act upon it. To refuse to accept this challenge of leadership is to stunt the growth of the Church and to run the risk of turning one's congregation into a "carefully protected corpse."[3]

The time is *now* for women to be bearers of the good news, to be prophets. Although the future is not our "natural" environment, nevertheless we are called to co-create it, to be agents of changes that humanize and liberate. "Their sons and daughters shall prophesy."[4] A prophet listens to the holy Spirit, is rooted in her contemporary situation, notes discrepancies between what the Spirit says and the living of it. Then she dares to speak words of loving rebuke which prepare the way for new forms and growth.

But growth is unpredictable! Belonging "inseparably to the Church's life and holiness,"[5] women Religious should grow, develop, and explore as the Church does! So then an unrealistic, over-secularized approach of viewing Religious life as another "career" doesn't "fit" the prophetic stance. Rather it should be seen as a religious event, an experience stretching across one's lifetime and witnessing to the mystery and sign of God's presence. Somehow an "experience of God" is involved. If such a faith experience is to perdure, then any "formation program" must provide generously the space for solitude, education, interpersonal experience, etc., to allow this to happen. It is an indispensable prerequisite for leadership.

The question is will woman be willing to provide the leadership demanded by today's needs? Will she accept responsibility with the total Church to "scrutinize the signs of the times and interpret them in the light of the gospel?"[6] Our attitude toward our prophets is ambivalent: we want their message of freedom, but we shrink from the price it demands. Who are these prophets? Often the young in our own communities, the "cries of the poor" listening for an "echo in our lives,"[7] the dispossessed, the voices of the past, our own founders. . . . The "word of the Lord" comes from unexpected sources and it cannot be imprisoned. As the unknown, the untried, the unexplored become everyday experiences and risks for us, the challenge is to "penetrate the world with the gospel mandate."[8]

One simple approach as a launching pad is to re-examine the decrees/mandates of your own General Chapter of eight or ten years ago. With your knowledge of today's climate in the Church and in society, what do you wish your governing body had addressed in that chapter? How would you like to see things shaped three years hence? Ten years? Had today's realities been predicted ten years ago, I suspect few of us would have believed their fulfillment possible! Using the "Delphi Method" with a "council of the future" could also provide a creative group with a tool for making the future a present possibility.

Obviously there are no fixed blueprints — only human lives and the assurance that "God's Spirit is not absent from this development."[9] Living with questions will help to push the horizon of the future beyond our imagination. Some of this "pushing" will happen if our convictions are strong enough to trust that "God's power working in us can do more than we can ask or imagine."[10] So let's ask. Your answers could determine your future thrust. My comments are simply reflections and are not intended to provide *your* response.

Feminist Questions Determine Future Thrust

Are we convinced that participation by persons in decisions that affect their lives and destiny is a basic right and human need?

Yes. Some end-results then: Community policies will not be "shaped from above" but will be a composite of the discernment and decisions of all members. In both pre-planning stages of formation and the on-going process, administration personnel, grassroot Sisters, candidates, and any others affected will shape the decisions relating to courses, ministries, services, and programs that are adopted. In addition to these immediate operations women Religious will, by whatever measures are appropriate, work toward assuring equitable representation of women in all decision-making levels in the Church: parish, diocesan, and the Sacred Congregation of Religious, where laws are being enacted and policies adopted that concern both women and men. Principles of collegiality and subsidiarity will be operative on all levels, with mutual accountability a recognized constituent.

To attain the objectives of truth and justice, what "improvement in attitudes and widespread changes"[11] need to take place?

This Vatican II imperative gives scope for some "imagining." Women's rights (and men's) cannot be considered independent of human rights. Although masculinity and femininity are ways of being human, yet neither is a complete way by itself. There is always an implied relationship to the other and a share in the other. Humanness will blend the two, incorporate qualities of both in a person.

Feminists are men and women who believe that women are full human beings who should have full human rights in the Church and in society. Feminism is a path to fullness of humanization which men will also enjoy — but not while women are not free to realize their potential. This "freeing" experience calls for collaborative efforts. Communities will print their formation program for distribution among other groups to demonstrate how intercommunity cooperation is possible. Ways of utilizing the expertise of lay consultants, men and women, and the formative experiences with priests and men Religious, would also be indicated. Insights gained from such experience would enable "widespread changes" needed to eradicate stereotypes and injustices.

Why are training and competency in theological/religious studies indispensable for effective leadership?

Whatever we bring to other groups, individuals, or even to our national and international efforts will be whatever we have acquired through our own training and experience. An essential aspect of this will necessarily be the lifestyle of community living that is shared, where our life's values, concerns, and services can become known to others. Community living will provide a base for expressing solidarity in working for humanization. Struggles will be shared with one's community, hope will be generated, senior Sisters will "dream dreams" and younger ones will "see visions." All will celebrate life in this deciding and dreaming together.

This "training" needs to embody a living gospel vision, to acknowledge the giftedness that makes each person unique. Women must be free to express their own self-understanding and their own experience of God. Theological reflection should enable them to do this. In-depth study of social encyclicals, synod statements, and Church documents could be the basis of position papers for Chapters, thesis topics, experimental lifestyle suggestions. Solitude will be an essential ingredient so that "listening to the Spirit" may precede the transforming of structures of injustice.

Are corporate witness to justice and the call of individual members to witness to justice viewed as incompatible actions?

Members on all levels of any congregation should be involved in examining the social objectives of the congregation which define the investment objectives. It is important that all Sisters, including those in initial stages of formation, develop a social conscience and a strong sense of the community's responsibility. Membership on committees, such as fiscal concerns committees, should be open to all Sisters on all levels. In this way they can share in discerning the moral and social priorities in the community's investment policies.

In the process of this educational experience different inadequacies and inequities will become evident. The individual response will flow from community convictions about justice and should reenforce the community's stand rather than create a conflict. A massive amount of material is available for communities today on corporate investments. It should be an integral part of the formation programming.

The "questions" never end: How is consumerism opposed to gospel values? . . . How convinced are we that "Action on behalf of justice is a constitutive dimension of the preaching of the gospel''? [12] . . . What does the Council mean when it demands that every type of discrimination, including sex discrimination, is to be "overcome and eradicated as contrary to God's intent?"[13] . . . What action is required if we truly believe that interdependence in a global village is a Christian mandate? . . . Why is Pope Paul's exhortation to Religious to join in the political action of the world significant? . . . Religious development formation programs will be credible and meaningful only if the enablers and facilitators of the process as well as the participants are learning to "love the questions," and if they are living into creative answers. Our world is hungry for authentic prophets!

References

1. Walter M. Abbott, SJ, ed., "Gaudium et Spes," *Documents of Vatican II* (Guild Press, N.Y., 1966) p. 210 ff.
2. *Synod of Bishops* (1974 USCC, Washington, D.C.), p. 21.
3. Pope Pius XII, quoted by Joseph Gallen, SJ, *Authors on Renovation and Adaptation* (Woodstock College, 1958), p. 3.
4. Acts 2:17.
5. "Lumen Gentium," *Documents of Vatican II*, p. 75, No. 44.
6. "Gaudium et Spes," *op. cit.* p. 201, No. 4.
7. Pope Paul VI, *Apostolic Exhortation: Evangelica Testificatio* (USCC, Washington, D.C., 1971) p. 7.
8. *Ibid.*, p. 18.
9. "Gaudium et Spes," *op. cit.*, p. 226, No. 26.
10. Ephesians 3:20.
11. "Gaudium et Spes," *op. cit.*, p. 225, No. 26.
12. *Synod of Bishops*, 1971, quoted in *Quest for Justice* (Center of Concern, Washington, D.C.), p. 1.
13. "Gaudium et Spes," *op. cit.*, p. 228, No. 29.

Some Suggestions for Community Reflection on:

"Their . . . Daughters Shall Prophesy . . .": Leadership for Women in Church and Society?

"Feminists are men and women who believe that women are full human beings who should have full human rights in the Church and in society.

Feminism is a path of fullness of humanization which men will also enjoy, but not while women are not free to realize their potential."

- Share your experiences with feminists in your area.
- What is the role of consciousness-raising groups?
- How and when can the anger that oppressed women feel be channeled into creative actions in behalf of justice?
- "Our attitude toward our prophets is ambivalent: we want their message of freedom, but we shrink from the price it demands."
- How have you received the prophets in your community?
- How were you received when you took a prophetic stance in your community?
- How will the future Church benefit from the theologizing of women?
- In your community, what role do new members play in formulating policy for the community's religious development program?

26

Symbols and Liturgy

Nancy Swift, RCE

One of the problems we face today, and it is a very serious one, is the problem of unbelief. There are many causes for this; among them, we may note the following. Scientific and technological specialization have moved to center stage at the cost of religion. Religion, once the unifying rationale for all things, has been reduced to just one more department of human activity. The religions are now competing — whether this be in the form of "civil religion" or as a result of the impact of travel and mass media, and the introduction of Eastern religions into the West. There is also a change of lifestyle, where the emphasis is on the immediate. The rise of universal education has spread the gospel of positivism. Religion today does not seem to be interested in what people are doing in their everyday lives; we have sometimes turned it into a series of propositions and literal interpretations of the Bible. There is the confusion of institutional renewal within the larger upheaval of recurring change in society. And finally, we have the whole crisis of religious language. In short, we must recognize at least these secularizing influences upon our culture.

In particular, let us consider this problem of religious-belief crisis as it is manifested in the functional atheist. The functional atheist is one who does not experience the religious — who doesn't have religious experience. These functional atheists may be churchgoers, and they may attempt to pray. But they do not have a religious experience. And if this is the case, then nothing in liturgy and ritual is going to be meaningful. This is a very serious problem.

A few months ago, a number of professional American liturgists met to discuss common questions of liturgy, both from a pastoral and an academic point of view. All were in agreement that liturgical research and study (and hence formation) during the next few years will have to deal with two problems. Our work will have to be in the area of the nonverbal aspects of liturgy — the symbol (that is, gesture, sound, color, place, setting, movement, and so on); and second, we will have to give attention to helping people internalize what is going on at worship. This seems to be where we should be putting our resources.

As you know, we have completed the revision of the texts and rituals. As someone has said: "we have a new liturgical library."

What I would like to do is to share with you what I think is a valuable approach in looking at these two nonverbal aspects of liturgy, symbol and interiorization. I think that if we want our people to grow in their relationship with God this is where we should be operating.

What is happening today? There are a few presuppositions that I must make. First, it is a fact that there is an evolution of human consciousness; here, I rely upon the work of Eric Neumann — particularly his work: *Origins and History of Consciousness*. Neumann finds that human consciousness has evolved over the centuries and is an on-going reality. Our consciousness today is different from people's consciousness four or five centuries ago.

I also presuppose that an understanding of the laws of the human psyche is not a threat, but a help to faith. To investigate the psychic preconditions of the supernatural virtue of faith — to grasp the qualities that make it possible for the conscious to make a decision for Christianity, and for a life of faith to grow out of that decision — all of this is an aid to faith. And lastly, I presuppose that God operates within the laws of the human psyche. If God appears in human experience, in so doing he will neither violate his own Being nor the characteristic operation of the consciousness of his human subject. When God speaks to human beings, he speaks according to the laws of our own psychology. When I speak of the things that happen in our unconscious, I am looking at that as a place where the Spirit of God works — this is where we can look for signals of God within us — in the symbols and images that arise out of the unconscious.

I have noted some of the reasons for unbelief today. Now I would like to highlight one of these as the condition which characterizes our society today.

Literalizing Symbols

I am referring to the condition of *over-rationalism* in our Western civilization — we have developed our reason to a point that it now becomes of interest to believe.

There is also a reason outside of us for this unbelief: symbols and symbol systems can die — even images that embody our faith or the dogmas and creeds that encase what we believe. They can lose their meaning in proportion to their decreasing ability to quicken our awareness of the original experience of God out of which they arose. All the symbols that we use in ritual have come from an original experience of God, which is a numinous experience. And they can begin to lose their power to stir us and to waken us to this primal holy experience. One of the major reasons why this happens is that our present experience of God is not the same as people's experience many centuries ago.

We may find that the symbols we are accustomed to, those which speak to us of God, which act as a medium for our contact with the transcendent, are inadequate. Or, at least, that they do not evoke a response from us. Something is not quite right — something is not really taking hold of us. What we see happening is that our own experience of God, our religious experience, has changed and our traditional symbols have not. They no longer correspond to where we know God.

This may well be the case of those believers who feel uncomfortable in Christianity — it is not a question of unbelief. And some of these people are those who are in some way looking for the feminine attributes to be incorporated into God. The symbols we have do not speak to us of that. Another part of this problem — one that may cause unbelief — is that unless we can live and function symbolically we shall find it very difficult to have faith. Symbolic feeling is basic for Christianity; surely, symbol is necessary in order to enter into corporate worship.

By symbol and symbolic living, I mean a nonrational, figura-

tive constellation that points beyond itself to an unknown or un-
knowable objective reality and makes that reality perceptible to
us. But symbols are not rational vehicles. They function in the
nonrational category and connect us with a reality that we could
not know without symbol. The symbol can, at times, participate
in that reality — share a life with that reality.

But what happens when people begin to take symbols literally?
This has happened, and unfortunately, it still is happening. For
example, some who read the stories in the Old Testament about
the "Burning Bush" then try to analyze this phenomenon; or the
story of the gathering of the "manna"; some even try to figure
out just how large was the belly of the whale that Jonas was flung
into! This is what I call literalizing symbols.

We can also look at a symbol and try to explain it to our own rational mind. One contemporary example is the misunderstood
role of the commentator at our liturgical celebrations. The commentator today feels that every aspect of the ritual must be explained, rather than just letting us be there and experience the ritual activity. No, the overzealous commentator even tells us when
to sit, stand, and kneel. In this way, we rob the symbol of its
power. The symbol just will not speak to us that way. If we lit-
eralize and rationalize symbols, they will not transmit life — they
will be reduced to meaningless entities, and even to the absurd.

Jung and the Function of Symbols

There are both interior and exterior symbols — that is, we have
images within ourselves that come from the unconscious, and
images of things that are outside of us, such as trees, the moon
and the stars. There are also exterior symbols that have come from
the unconscious, images which we have projected. Artists have
created objects to correspond to those images. All of these symbols can function as a means to link us to realities that we could
not know otherwise. And they are very necessary for our belief.

I would like now to turn to what I believe is an approach
toward grasping what happens in the human psyche. Here, I turn
to the theory of symbol of Carl Jung. While Jung did not work out
all the answers, his research does give us a system whereby we can
begin to understand the functioning of symbol.

Jung describes the map of the human psyche: it is made up of energy, psychic energy — life force. There is an area of consciousness, an area of the personal unconscious, and then, the collective unconscious or the objective psyche. Consciousness is focused in what Jung calls the ego — the center of consciousness. The personal unconscious is that part of the unconscious which contains all the things that I have put there — those things that have come from my experience, both things I can recall and things I have suppressed and repressed.

But Jung's greatest contribution is what he calls the collective unconscious. This contains not my dreams or ideas or feelings that I have collected during my lifetime, but the memories of the race. In this collective unconscious are the images and symbols that are born in us — part of human nature. And in fact, Jung believed that they were put there by God. The collective unconscious is an inheritance given to us.

These different qualities of the psyche are composed or structured in opposites. These are some of the polarities, for example: conscious versus unconscious, thinking abilities versus feeling, sensing versus intuiting; the emotional side of me as contrasted with the rational; the intuitive way of knowing as contrasted with the inductive and logical capacity I have. The physical, sensual part of me is in tension with the spiritual and the intellectual; my ability to perceive things as a whole is contrasted with my ability to separate things and to discriminate.

The symbols that function as a summary of all these polarities Jung calls the basic polarity of masculine qualities versus feminine qualities. This, of course, has nothing to do with man or woman; it is the basic polarity that is in each man and in each woman. For Jung, psychic health meant the reconciliation of all these opposites — not in the sense of getting rid of the polarities, and especially not to polarize them into destructive tendencies and tensions, but rather to integrate them. It is the interplay of these polarities that gives us psychic life.

Jung also believed that the psyche has a capacity to generate images from itself which can reconcile these opposites. In fact, these come out of the psyche but we cannot demand or program them — they simply happen. They are given to us (and in theological terms, these are manifestations of grace). The holy Spirit will, at his own time and if we attend to what is going on inside

us, release in us through the unconscious images that will reconcile these opposites. Jung believed, then (in theological terms),
that the image of God arrives in us when our true *self* emerges.

Again, I go back to the masculine and feminine that are in each
of us. It is a fact that great numbers of people in our society
overstress the qualities that we associate with masculinity — for
example, rational, logical thinking, the ability to discriminate,
and so on. The feminine would be more an instinctual perception
of the whole. An example may help to illustrate this: in the
human eye — the organ by which we have sight — we know that
we have two kinds of vision, peripheral and then a more centered,
focused vision. In the one case, we know what is going on all
around us, while in the other we can focus on one object. The
feminine way of knowing is more like the peripheral vision, this
sense of the whole, and the focus vision is the masculine way of
knowing. We need both kinds of vision, and a healthy person
needs both ways of knowing, but it is quite a task to integrate
them.

What we find from these studies is that the feminine quality of
consciousness, or the feminine mode of perception, is necessary
for the reception of religious symbols. In fact, it seems to be a
very important avenue for symbolic functioning — and in itself it
is nonrational and nonverbal. This is a very serious statement to
make: that the primary way we can contact God is not through rational thinking (which puts us in contact with the surrogate God)
but through the intuitive, the sensual way of knowing, which
Jung called the feminine way of knowing. And the problem with
us is that our society has reached the culmination point in the development of rationalism, of being clear, of thinking logically —
our whole scientific methodology depends on that kind of thinking. I think that one of the problems with belief today is the fact
that we have *undervalued* the feminine mode of being and the
feminine way of knowing. Both men and women have undervalued this.

Feminine Elements in Christian Symbolism

But this is beginning to change; we are undergoing a very gradual
but fundamental change of consciousness. There are many signs
of this: for example, the human development movement, the

women's movement, the number of publications that emphasize bringing us back to our feelings. All these things manifest significant change in basic attitudes. People today are beginning to talk about their experience of God. Perhaps some of this is an influence of the charismatic movement wherein shared prayer is central. Whatever the reason, we do see that people are speaking more freely about their religious experiences. Maybe we are becoming more at ease with this whole side of ourselves that responds to God. We are beginning to accept our emotional life and we value it; we are not so embarrassed to listen to people who share with us their experience of God.

If it is true that the primary way of knowing God is through the nonverbal, through symbol — symbols that do not appeal to our reason — then what about our religious ritual and liturgy? What are some of the implications of all this for liturgy?

Let us remember that ritual provides a religious experience which allows a worshipper to assume a new identity and through ritual to clarify his/her own identity. It is a religious experience that prompts the worshipper to consider who he/she is in the eyes of God and the Church. Ritual of itself is like a work of art in that it is not utilitarian. It is like a magnificent tapestry on the wall — it is to be appreciated and valued, but not "used." This is very hard for the rational mind to accept. And yet, ritual is a symbol; and this means that the more we get in touch with the artist and the poet in ourselves, the greater capacity we will have to worship.

Ritual, if it is strong, exists in a special kind of time — we could call it "time outside time." Unless ritual provides us with an atmosphere which holds us into timelessness, then we really do not appreciate it. If, for example, our liturgies do not take us out of the mainstream of events, the everyday rhythm, the banal, then we can be pretty sure the ritual will not be effective. A truly good ritual can cast us into "illo tempore" — into that time of primal origins — and through the ritual we celebrate the original events again here and now. The ability to appreciate this "special moment," this "illo tempore," is a feminine attribute — it is part of the feminine side of our psyche. Hence, the more we can get in touch with this particular capacity, the more we shall appreciate ritual.

Ritual, as we have said, is built of symbols and symbol systems. We must face the fact that in using symbols and expecting them to speak, we must let them speak with their own power. We should not try to explain the symbol, but let it speak for itself. If we expect symbols (whether they be gesture, movement, art, music or people themselves) to trigger the emotional energy that is inside us, then we have to give them the strength and room to speak for themselves.

I think we can look within our own tradition and find those feminine symbols which will speak to us of God. For example, in the Old Testament we read (Isaiah 48,15):

> Can a woman forget the child of her womb?
> Even if she forget, yet I will not forget you.

In the New Testament, the story of Jesus weeping over Jerusalem:

> How often have I longed to gather your children, as a hen gathers her brood under her wings; but you would not let me.

Even in our doctrines of faith (e.g., Genesis 1, 27ff):

> God created man in his own image; in the image of God he created him; male and female he created them.

What is this image of God? The creation of man in the image of God, the "imago dei," can be understood psychologically as the capacity to produce symbols that center and unify psychic opposites and depict man's yearning for direct experience of his relation to a source of being beyond himself. Theologically, the "imago dei" has been interpreted to mean the creation of man as one who has the capacity to relate to his creator, although this capacity has either been diminished or even lost as a result of sin.

"Male and female he created them." This has been interpreted in a very interesting way by Ann Ullanov. She says:

> God's image is to be found in the polarity of male and female and the primary concretization of the covenant between God and his creature is to be found in the relationship of man and woman.

This interpretation is significant because it makes clear the essential importance of the feminine. If the feminine is neglected, or is misunderstood as a second-best category of human sexuality, then not only is the fullness of human being damaged but the relation of the human and the divine is damaged as well.

Other tenets of Christianity could be used to bring alive within our own tradition this feminine side of our nature: the crucifixion, the redemption, the function of the Holy Spirit and of the Virgin Mary. Perhaps the symbolism of Mary can be translated into a modern study of the feminine, opening our eyes to the depth of the religious symbol as well as to what it reveals about the feminine. In the materiality of Mary we find represented the possibility of human individuation, worked out through the successive reconciliations of opposites that are mainly symbolized in terms of the masculine-feminine polarity.

Mary is just one of many expressions of the feminine in Christian symbolism and in the Bible that have not been sufficiently explored. We have the example of Ruth, and the other Marys of the New Testament. All these are figures to be examined and explored in order to make explicit the feminine elements in Christian symbolism.

Jung's contribution to the psychology of the feminine will be very useful to all involved in formation. If we want our people to grow in their relationship with God we must begin to deal seriously with the nonverbal aspects of liturgy: i.e., symbol and interiorization.

Some Suggestions for Community Reflection on:

Symbols and Liturgy

- Liturgists and formation personnel must focus on the non-verbal aspects of liturgy and upon helping persons internalize what is happening at worship. How are Religious communities presently focusing on these aspects of liturgical formation?

Comment on the following statements:
- Symbols can lose their power to put us in contact with God.
- Unless we can live and function symbolically, we shall find it very difficult to have faith.
- Some believers feel uncomfortable now in Christianity because they do not have symbols which adequately speak to them of the feminine attributes of God.

- Primarily, we contact God through intuition, which is the sensual way of knowing, the feminine way of knowing. Both men and women in our culture have undervalued the feminine mode of being and the feminine way of knowing. Share with others any changes of consciousness in this regard which you have noted in yourself, in others close to you, in your community, in your family and in those to whom you minister, and finally in those who minister to you.
- How have you been affected by the new rite of profession and the revisions of your own community's ceremonials.
- Comment on how you think Religious are now experiencing the new rite of penance.

27

Formation for Social Justice, Fad or Mandate: A Young Religious Wonders

Rhonda Meister, SP

A friend recently shared the following image with me: wheels of a car whirling round and round at breakneck speed, and then beginning to slow down ever so gradually until they turned gently and with a very smooth and steady rhythm. This image speaks very forcefully to me of our journey since Vatican II. There was the frenzied whirl of the initial changes, and the chaos of many skid marks. Of late, however, there is an almost imperceptible slowing and deepening. The cadence is more steady now, and there is a sense of approaching balance. It is beginning to feel as if the wheels are moving us in a continual downward and outward rhythm of reflection-action-reflection. As the wheels of my own being steady, the repetitious cry that keeps rising is that of the oppressed, the exploited and the alienated — the two-thirds of the world that is hungry.

Are Formation Personnel Really Listening to the Church?

Since Vatican II there has been increased emphasis on social justice, and urgent calls for Christians to become involved in efforts to simplify their lives and to act more justly. Documents such as *Peace on Earth, The Progress of People, A Call to Action*, and *Justice in the World*, signal a powerful new thrust in Christian life.

198

They call us beyond the boundaries of family, neighborhood, and nation. They call us to a global vision, to assume responsibility for all those in need. They seek our involvement in changing the very structures of oppression and injustice. There is an urgency and radicalness about these documents that somehow continues to elude us as Christians and as Religious communities. We still spend so much of our energy debating whether social action and involvement is just a passing whim, or whether it is a binding mandate. It seems that continued and excessive debate on this subject is a luxury afforded only to the elite. The oppressed and the starving can afford such energy only for action.

Perhaps the strongest reply to this debate is found in the synodal document, *Justice in the World.* In the introduction, the bishops state:

> Action on behalf of justice and participation in the transformation of the world fully appear to us as a *constitutive* dimension of the preaching of the gospel or, in other words, of the Church's mission for the redemption of the human race and its liberation from every oppressive situation (my emphasis).

It is impossible to overestimate the importance of this statement in the light of its theological and pastoral significance. When the bishops speak of "action on behalf of justice" as a constitutive dimension of the ministry of the Church, it is important to reflect upon the full meaning of this phrase. Traditionally, the constitutive functions of the Church have been the celebration of the sacraments and the preaching of the gospel. Thus, by their synodal statement, the bishops have affirmed that work for justice is *essential* to the Church, and relates to its innermost nature and call. In essence, then, it is equally as important for the Church to engage in work for social justice every day as it is to provide for the celebration of the Eucharist or the preaching of the gospel. Father Bryan Hehir, in his paper, "The Ministry for Justice," comments on this constitutive dimension.

> Historically, whenever the constitutive tasks of the Church (word and sacrament) could not be performed or were not being faithfully fulfilled we feared for the life of the Church; today if the work for justice is not being carried on in an area of the Church, we should again fear for the life of the Church.

The ramifications of this statement are at once frightening and challenging, unsettling and yet hopeful. For it would appear that the action sought is more than the performance of charitable works, because basically it involves a commitment to change unjust social structures systematically.

It strikes me that this message of justice should fall on particularly fertile ground when heard by those working in formation, and those actually in the formation process. For both formation personnel and the young Religious have an important part in shaping the future community, and a concurrent responsibility for helping to build a just world. Yet as I reflect upon my own life in relation to the responsibility for "acting in behalf of justice," I am confronted with many questions — questions that I would like to share with you about the formation process. These questions arise from my own search to respond more fully to the Lord, and I address them not only to you, but also to myself.

Are Formation Personnel Impeding the Church's Call to Justice?

How many of our formation programs place equal emphasis upon social justice, sacramental life, and the gospel? Is there an expectation on the part of formation personnel and the Religious community that those in formation will work actively in the realm of social justice? Is this expectation articulated? Is it considered as important for the Religious to be involved in attempting to transform unjust structures as to attend liturgy and to reflect upon the Word? Do formation personnel consider it their Christian responsibility to work for social justice actively? In the education program for the young Religious, is adequate time allowed for a study of social theology? In the periodic evaluations of the young Religious, are they called to accountability in terms of their commitment to social justice?

I wonder how often instead of the expectation there is a fear, a caution, or sometimes even a lack of support on the part of the formation personnel or the larger community? This may be expressed in a number of ways. Sometimes it is a masked perfectionism which compels one to wait to act until the path is absolutely clear, and there is no doubt as to the right choice. This path seems to exclude the faith and trust elements completely. Sometimes there is the conspicuous absence of anything even remotely resembling justice involvement — a type of selective vision. Other times, the action is very rationally pushed into the future, and is articulated in the following way: "When you get yourself together, then will be the time to become involved in a ministry for justice." These seem to be stances which each of us can find ourselves in at one time or another in our lives.

Peter Henriot, in his paper, "The Public Dimension of the Spiritual Life of the Christian: The Problem of Simultaneity," deals with this latter stance. He calls into question our tendency to view the individual, the interpersonal, and the public dimensions of the human person separately.

> These are not three separate and distinct dimensions so much as three moments in our perception of a single reality, or three interrelated and interpenetrated aspects. Thus the identity of a human person is inadequately situated outside a consideration of all three *simultaneously* (my emphasis).

Henriot points out that in speaking of the spiritual life we have traditionally tended to focus on the individual dimension, with some attention given to the interpersonal. What he is emphasizing is the need to speak of the spiritual life in terms of all three dimensions simultaneously. This type of approach would void the rationale of "getting oneself together, and then becoming involved." So much has been written about relating to the total human person, and yet there still remains the temptation to separate — to continue a dichotomy between prayer and action. Henriot states that:

> as important as it may be to see this commitment to act for social justice as being a consequence of growth in true spirituality, it is even more important to understand and to practice . . . this commitment as being simultaneous to the growth process itself.

Internalization of this concept of simultaneity seems to offer a way of enabling our commitment to justice to move from the realm of principle to practice.

Is Our Theology of Community Futuristic?

The whole issue of simultaneity calls into question our current presentation of other essentials of Religious life, such as community and the vows. What is our theology of community? Does it relate to the international community? Is it built on our need to grow in global interdependence? Does it challenge us to be mindful of the resource shortage? Does our presentation of community lead us to a sense of solidarity with all persons? Have we so internalized this sense that we have personally responded to the hunger crisis? Have we assumed responsibility for changing our food consumption patterns?

It seems that basic to our ability to become committed to social justice is a grasp of the concept of global interdependence. Our presentation of community would seem lacking if it fails to develop a global vision. We must experience and internalize so that our actions and our style of life may drastically affect the lives of people we will never meet. We must assume responsibility for those of our actions and our excesses which deprive others of the sustenance to live. When we speak of a theology of community, it must somehow connect and relate to the fact that, as Americans, we represent 6% of the world's population and yet consume 40% of its resources.

In *Justice in the World,* the bishops address themselves to this incongruity between words and lived witness, and speak of the loss of credibility that will be ours if we fail to meet the challenge of effective action.

> While the Church is bound to give witness to justice, it recognizes that anyone who ventures to speak to people about justice must first be just in their eyes. For unless the Christian message of love and justice shows its effectiveness through action in the cause of justice in the world, it will only with difficulty gain credibility with the men of our times.

Can We Risk the Experience of Jesus?

Throughout this paper I have focused on questions which are confronting us as we journey into the future. However, it will not be the questions or even the structures themselves which will make the difference, but rather the interior change of heart which must take place within us. The answers lie within us and we must risk letting them surface. Are we willing to risk deep engagement with Jesus in which we become aware of and experience ourselves as Peter did: sent by Jesus to be servant? There is a depth change in the quality of our commitment to justice when we allow Jesus to anoint and wash our feet. We have then experienced ourselves commissioned as his servant, so that we in turn may wash the feet of others. As servants, we are aware that we cannot be satisfied with the status quo. We know that God is always calling us beyond who we are and where we are. The wheels continue rolling with a deepening steadiness and gentling rhythm. *Signs of Hope: the Way of Life of the Sisters of Providence* articulates verbally what the wheel images:

> The on-going drama of life is unfinished and full of new horizons; we are involved in forging a world that is always new, a future that is always discovering us.

This document challenges me and my Sisters in community to build tomorrows of justice and hope. Hopefully, all new or revised rules will challenge Religious to simplify their lives and to act more justly.

Some Suggestions for Community Reflection on:

Formation for Social Justice, Fad or Mandate: A Young Religious Wonders

- Share an experience you have had of being changed by a person you were teaching.
- In what ways have documents such as *Peace on Earth*, the *Progress of People*, *A Call to Action*, and *Justice in the World* influenced your formation program and policies?

If you were a young Religious, how might you feel upon hearing the following from Sisters in your community or from those in formation and leadership positions?

- "When you get yourself together, then you may get involved in social justice."
- "You are only trying to get attention by becoming involved in social justice."
- "You really are not ready to get involved. Wait until the community is more ready and until you have more knowledge and experience."

Share an experience:

- in which Jesus washed your feet and commissioned you as his servant;
- in which you washed the feet of another in the name of Jesus.

Part III   Joshua-time

The future Christians are yearning for is something that is to happen and at the same time is already happening now. Christians must balance this tension between hoping for the fulfillment of the future kingdom and creating the present kingdom through participation in the movements of modern culture and society. The God of promise is ever calling into question the "new worlds" men design. In response, Christians are called continually to criticize, to transform their times.

Signs of Hope: Way of Life of the Sisters of Providence, Holyoke, MA

In these final two chapters the editors offer the personal reflections that emerged from their experience of the CARA Symposium and the Formation Futureshop. Ruth McGoldrick, SP, Executive Director of the Sister Formation Conference, in a penetrating article delineates the characteristics of the prophet so needed in Religious life today. She emphasizes flexibility, innovative insight, and future-orientation. Coping with today's complexities calls us to greater creative interdependence. "The Gatherings of the Resourceful." Practical methods for realizing our combined potentialities are reviewed. Cassian J. Yuhaus, CP, founder of the International Institute for Religious and CARA's Religious Life Program Coordinator, addresses himself to the optionizing process needed for today's communities of Religious in order to properly evaluate, prudently reflect, and courageously decide courses of action toward a planned future. He believes all religious institutes throughout the Church can be classified in one of three categories: new, renewing, diminishing. Each category confronts a unique series of challenges. Successful coping with these challenges depends upon the institution's use of a two-fold resource, both limited, both essential: time and talent. No community need stumble into a future no one expected and no one wants. He concludes by examining three fundamental tests by which a community may gauge its progress or regress.

Joshua-time

(Reflections of a participant)

I

spring
  is
  in the air
winter
  has not yet passed
  but
  it cannot
  last
for
spring
is gently piercing
  the
      cold
      black
      night
  with
      sun
      power
      might
and
breathes
unmistakably
  new life
  new light

II

We are leaven
  —no longer
  foundational
  institutional
  impositional
      outnumbering
      power

  —but now
  small
  life-sacrificing
  catalysts
      energizing
      healing
      enabling
      another
      to flower.

III

the seed is dying
the desert is on the verge of bloom
the purging wilderness has
  lead the pilgrims to the tomb
  where stripped in death
  the anawim emerge closer
  to the burning bush
  ready and waiting
  in communion:
      it's Joshua-time
      new covenant
      deeper union

Mary Frances Reis, BVM
Office of Ministry
Sisters of Charity, BVM

28

"Gatherings of the Resourceful" — Connecting with the Future

Ruth McGoldrick, SP

Bicentennial planners are focusing upon our nation's past, present, and future through the themes of heritage, festival, and horizons. The National Leadership Board of the Sister Formation Conference decided to center its bicentennial programming on the horizons theme — shaping the future. This focus was chosen to forward the spirit of the pioneers in the Conference — a spirit of "boldness, endurance, and readiness to risk."

The Futureshop on Formation, which was held at the Mercy Generalate from September 28 to October 2, 1975, was a national gathering of resourceful, future-oriented women Religious, women who have moved beyond a preoccupation with adaptation, and even beyond a concentration on the renewal of Religious life. These women are in touch with all those who are projecting and shaping a new global world built upon interdependence and communion. They are women who are willing to risk — women with intuition, imagination, vision, and values.

These women Religious are exploring ways to share the experience and expertise they have in the areas of personal, spiritual, and organizational renewal. They are aware of the power in this kind of resourcefulness, a power that could change both the Church and society. Furthermore, they intend to use this power in the service of the gospel and of the poor. Fortunately, most formation teams have such future-conscious, prophetic women in their midst. Futureshop participants showed the same creativity and courage as did the women in leadership and formation positions prior to and after the Council — the women who pioneered the Sister Formation movement.

Future-Consciousness in Our Religious Life

Prophets are persons in the culture who are future-conscious, persons of vision. Such persons are able to "walk newly in old ways," for they are surprisingly creative in their ability to live in what we would describe as pilgrim and paschal ways. It is characteristic of prophetic pilgrims always to be reflecting, remembering, and retracing their footsteps in order to gain deeper insight into the present and to be in touch with intuitions that will carry them forward into the future. It is characteristic of paschal persons to see and give life in "death" situations, to undertake seemingly hopeless tasks and often to accomplish the impossible.

Prophets are so caught up with seeking and seeing reality that they refuse to give undue attention to things of lesser moment. They are typically unconcerned about money, power, or prestige, for they value deeper realities such as justice, peace, and unity. The culture's prophets tend toward community in order to keep their vision clear and their values practical in rituals, actions, and lifestyle.

Religious life attracts prophetic persons, uncompromising in their vision and values. We know from recent experience with renewal that no community is able to create such prophets, no matter how beautiful its documents nor how flexible and sophisticated its structures and formation programs. It is the prophetic person who continually creates and re-creates the community and its way of life.

All Religious are prophetic to some degree, for all are called to live in three time dimensions at once — the past, the present, and the future. We know also that some Religious can navigate back and forth in these time spans rather easily, while others live mostly in one dimension. Every Religious community, as every culture, has persons who live out the attitudes and values of each historical age as well as of each stage of spiritual development. A few Religious live mostly in the past and can offer the community the memory of its rich heritage. The majority of Religious live in the present, keeping the community anchored to its daily life and ministries. Another few are called to live adventurously towards the future, struggling with and testing out new theologies, life-styles, and models of relating and ministering. Although all journey occasionally into the other two less familiar time spans, the more prophetic and integrated persons can make the journeys in time more easily, swiftly, and with greater delight.

Some Religious are also gifted with more religious insight and motivation that others. These are the more resourceful ones, called to challenge the community to keep moving into the future, moving in the direction of Religious creativity and fidelity to gospel values and vision. These prophets are best described as paradoxical, for they live with greater ease the gospel paradox — the paschal dyings and risings. Though on the frontiers of religious experience, they are relaxed in the midst of activity and always exploring new ways to see God and to express their commitment. They have so internalized the vision and values of Jesus that they are able to move freely and hopefully into the unknown future. Because for them gospel values re-enforce each other, these are the Religious who experience the least amount of conflict between prayer and ministry or between community and ministry. They are the contemplatives-in-action, who welcome change and diversity.

Prophetic persons are open, gifted with creative ideas and options for the future. They quickly identify with the young and with other future-oriented persons in the culture, seeking communion with all who have creative energy. These prophetic persons see beneath current crises the seeds of a new society not built on destructive values such as competition and exploitation. Since they understand and identify with the Church's struggle to enter a new era, they are quick to encourage any leadership the Church takes and just as quick to prod the Church when it is not modeling gospel values in its structures. They are to the Church what the Church must be for the world — a sign of hope pointing to a future world-in-communion.

Networks of the Future

Futurist Alvin Toffler has a sense of the value and workings of process. In "What Is Anticipatory Democracy?" (the October

1975 issue of *The Futurist*), Toffler stated that democratic political systems face two crucial problems: a lack of future-consciousness and a lack of citizen participation. His solution is anticipatory democracy — a process designed to cope with both of these problems simultaneously. (Anticipatory Democracy [AD] is a way of reaching decisions that determine our future.) We know that management-by-crisis is not working and that bureaucracies are obsolete, thus a whole new set of participatory institutions is necessary both in our churches and in society. To date, Religious communities have taken the lead, for Religious communities who intend to survive the present religious and cultural transitions are already into processes aimed at bringing about the involvement of all members in decision-making and planning for the future.

Both Religious and futurists have much to learn from the dynamic and intuitive ways of Brother Roger, the Prior of Taizé. In calling and preparing for the World-Wide Council of Youth, "a council of things to come," he initiated a global process that is still unfolding step by step. For "American" minds that look for instant success, this long process is most inefficient; yet it is one of the few projects that is captivating the imaginations and hearts of youth. Brother Roger sensed the hope of youth for a new vision and a new project which would bind them to Christ, a commitment that would free the energies within them in a burst of creativity that would liberate the world. The Council of Youth is not a meeting or a movement, but an *event* in the Church that will live for several years. It attracts youth who are thirsting for communion with God and others.

It is evident that youth, futurists, and Religious prophets all dream of a future world-in-communion. Young persons in cells on every continent are living the Council of Youth, while futurists are meeting in local, national, and international chapters and numerous Religious are living in formative communities throughout the world. All of these future-oriented communities are characterized by an attitude of exploration. Dotting our small planet today are new and vast networks of future-conscious communities, testing new styles of living and working together. They need to communicate with one another and with all citizens. Toffler uses the analogy of the human eye to describe what the Sister

Formation Conference sought to do in its Futureshop by "gathering the resourceful."

> We need people who can see straight ahead and deep into the problem. Those are the experts. But we also need peripheral vision and experts are generally not very good at providing peripheral vision. And I would suggest that what we need is a whole set of new ways of relating "experts" — people who have PhD's and specialized expertise — and lay experts — those who are extremely expert about their little piece of the environment, which may turn out to be very important to the rest of us as well (*The Futurist*, October, 1975).

Future-conscious Religious know that for their own growth they need to belong to many formative communities. They also experience their own on-going formation as a process of continually journeying to an outward kingdom that is already within. Such insight into such gospel paradox comes only from living at a deep faith level. Therefore, the person, the message, and the promise of Jesus must penetrate all who live in formative communities, so that they continually see with new vision and act out of hearts always in the process of conversion. Eventually, new members learn in their formative faith communities what it means to live in hope and in process. They learn not to set up useless dichotomies, but to live with the tension of paradox that will keep them in motion, future-oriented. In time, new members come to know what the older members have learned through years of prayer and experience: that fidelity in Religious life is both gift and process.

Future-oriented persons who are concerned about how to keep themselves in process, are experimenting with ways of going to the deepest center of self. Zen, yoga, mind control, transcendental meditation are evoking great interest. Two other future-oriented methods (methods that bring persons to the place of inner wisdom where past, present, and future meet in dialogue) are the Intensive Journal and Centering Prayer.

Futuristic Methods of Religious Practice — Two Models

Ira Progoff, the founder of Dialogue House, has developed a comprehensive growth program. The Sister Formation Conference has worked with Dr. Progoff since 1974, sponsoring Intensive Journal/Process Meditation workshops throughout the country and encouraging Religious to become trained as Journal

Consultants. The Journal Method puts a person in touch with the movement, the unifying threads, the continuity of one's life — its paschal rhythms.

Each person is introduced to a specially structured workbook called the Intensive Journal during the first journal workshop. A person is then able to explore the callings and meanings of life in privacy or while working in the supportive atmosphere of a group. It is in the interplay of the exercises and techniques that a momentum builds deep within which propels the individual forward and outward. The method is valuable in initial and on-going formation because it works toward the growth of the whole person in a way that is inherently spiritual. Through the method a Religious is able to unfold potentials in accord with basic Religious commitment, even reinforcing that commitment by gaining access to untapped resources and potential within one's own depths. She or he is able to structure life goals progressively, at one's own pace and on one's own terms, no matter what the individual level of sophistication. The journal thus provides an active instrument and individual techniques for an open-ended and ongoing program of personal or communal development.

The journal method also includes a special technique called Process Meditation. Meditation here is understood to be a way of meditating between one's inner and outer life. The ability to do this helps the needed integration we spoke of earlier — the ease with which prophetic persons can live in time spans and at deep levels and still be actively present in their outer life and activity. Unlike other methods which take persons to the deep center of self, the Intensive Journal does provide built-in safeguards. Because it is based on the self-balancing principle and is non-judgmental, it poses no psychological dangers. This is an effective method for a person who wishes to work intensely in his or her own life either privately, with a spiritual director or Journal consultant, or in a group.

Presently the Journal has three main sections. The Time dimension deals with ways of getting in touch with and moving forward in one's own life history. The Depth dimension has exercises and techniques which provide a way to work with imagery, dreams, inner wisdom figures, and prayer experiences. The Dialogue dimension provides ways to dialogue with self, with other persons either living or dead, and with significant events or relationships. Once a person is introduced to the method, the Intensive Journal becomes a friend that responds to and carries forward the creativity and rhythms of the person who befriends it.

Centering Prayer

Two Trappists from St. Joseph's Abbey in Spencer, Massachusetts are teaching a method that satisfies the needs of some who quest for a deeper spiritual life. The method is being presented at workshops for small groups of men and women Religious throughout the country. In the pilot Practical Religious Experience Workshops sponsored by the Religious Life Committee of the Conference of Major Superiors of Men in 1974 and 1975, four elements in the workshops emerged as particularly helpful: spiritual partnerships, sacred reading, shared prayer, and the prayer of centering. Follow-up days are encouraged to create new support groups. The prayer is named "centering prayer" from the teaching of Thomas Merton that the way we come to God is by going into our deepest center and there passing into God. This centering prayer is a simple method for entering into contemplative prayer. Although spiritual leaders have consistently stated that Religious should be ready for contemplative prayer by the time of profession, formation personnel have either failed to take them seriously or have lacked a method to achieve this.

Coincidentally, both Dr. Progoff and the two Trappists, Basil Pennington, OCSO, and William Menninger, OCSO, are developing insights from the author of the *Cloud of Unknowing*. Both of these new methods of religious practice are practical, structured, on-going methods which make use of ancient as well as contemporary wisdom. They both appeal to those who like to explore both inner and outer space — the young and the future-conscious. Tapes are available on both methods.

Projecting Preferable Futures

Future-conscious persons must come together to share intuitions, so that all of us will be able to see more deeply and comprehensively. It was the sense of the planners of the Futureshop that something hopeful and exciting would happen if there were a dialogue among resourceful persons in: adult education, emerging ministries, futuristics, and formation. We felt that registrants would be persons who had reflected upon the religious and cultural transitions which are generating such great tensions, persons ready to project new images and models for the future. Planners of the Futureshop sense that more turbulence is ahead, because there is so much pent-up emotion and so much frustration about the future. They wish to devise a way to channel some of this energy into projecting alternative futures.

Toffler is pleading with all futurists to help in finding ways to "destandardize, decentralize, deconcentrate, descale, and democratize planning." Formation personnel must listen and respond to Toffler's appeal. Only those communities who have an active sense of providence will move into the future. To live creatively as a Christian and as a futurist one must rest one's hopes upon the providence of God while working actively and imaginatively to invent a better future.

There can be a more just society if future-conscious persons act quickly and choose wisely. In this era of communications, vast changes in society can come about in less than ten years. It is also a fact today that the impact of technological change is lessening to the point where we will have a brief respite from future shock. Now is an opportune time for Religious to make a significant contribution to the progress of peoples. Religious can take the lead in finding ways to heal the great wounds in our society and in creating new models for living gospel values in the coming decades. Carl Edward Braaten states it well:

> It is hoped that the renewal of the Christian vision of the eschatological future of man and his world and the qualities of its promises and hopes will commingle with the models of the future which are now being constructed by an elite corps of futurologists in every country. The role of the compassionate religion is simply to keep the spotlight on the human face of man in every discussion, in every experiment, in every scheme that futurologists devise — especially the human face of those who are poor, powerless, and futureless — so that the least of all our fellow beings may be liberated for a fulfilling life on earth.

Future Consciousness in Formation Personnel

The hope was that the Futureshop would stimulate formation personnel to sponsor Futureshops in their local and regional com-

munities. We have feedback already that this is happening.
Though there is still a need for some formation personnel to continue their involvement in community renewal, they must begin
to move beyond this into the universities, the marketplaces, the
poverty areas where the new ideas, models and values are being
tossed around and tested.

Much literature is available on futuristics, especially from the
World Future Society and scores of other futures organizations
that exist. Some Religious communities are following the lead of
business, government, and education in appointing in-house futurists. Many communities have established commissions and sec-
retariats on the future. The School Sisters of St. Francis are sharing not only their very excellent workbook entitled *Pages of the
Future*, but also a group of resource persons.

Far too many community planners and formation coordinators
are still unfamiliar with the whole art and science of androgogy —
the principles of adult education. The desire for help in planning
continuing education programs was the need that surfaced as the
greatest during the Futureshop. This same need surfaced earlier
in the response the SFC had to its 1975 On-Going Formation
Workshops, where over 400 planners participated in six workshops held throughout the country. No person involved in formation work today can afford to remain unfamiliar with current
educational trends and terminology. Such concepts as the seamless
curriculum and the future-focused role image have important
implications for formation coordinators. Excellent resource material is also necessary and easily available in women's studies, and
in emerging concepts and models of ministry.

In the last decade well over 100 new Religious communities
have come into existence in the United States. Religious in all
parts of the country belong to groups experimenting with new
lifestyles and ministries. All of this movement points to the great
need there is for more frequent "gatherings of the resourceful."

A New Model for Ministerial Formation in the Future

To move the Futureshop dialogues forward another step, I would
like to propose for discussion and testing a model for ministerial
formation. Imagine the day in the not too distant future when
there will be no more seminaries or formation centers. Even the

transitional intercommunity formation programs will also have served their purpose. Imagine regional and national ministerial learning communities, open to all who wish to begin or to continue their formal preparation for ministry. Such learning communities would welcome men and women of all ages, in all stages of life-long formation, and from all traditions.

To connect with the future, Religious must have an active sense of providence: the ability to wait upon God's designs while at the same time working imaginatively to create a future. In this future world-in-communion, all in the Church will be prepared and encouraged to minister, each according to his or her gifts.

29

Optionizing and the Future of Religious Life

Cassian Yuhaus, CP

When CARA decided to observe its tenth anniversary by offering a series of symposia relating to its work and the needs for research and planning in various areas of Church life, it was inevitable that Religious life would place high on the agenda. This was due to two facts. Not only have Religious institutes greatly encouraged and supported CARA from its very inception but no other area of Church life has responded so totally and so energetically to the challenge of renewal issuing from Vatican II. The numerous studies on Religious life at CARA reveal the courageous and vigorous work of Religious for effective renewal and their deep and abiding concern for the future. Other areas of Church life do not manifest an equal concern or effort.

An invitation to work with the Sister Formation Conference was indeed welcome and providential. CARA warmly responded to the opportunity to share and to learn. For me the learning experience proved to be more important and valuable than the sharing, although that also was significant. The original idea of the Futureshop as the "gathering of the resourceful" has great meaning for the future of Religious life. The dynamic employed in evoking new talent, exploring potential and stimulating multiple responses was in itself of inestimable value. This served to underscore our interdependence. It affirmed once again the truth of the paradox that the only way we can achieve independent strength and existence is through genuine interdependence.

It is no longer possible for any single institute to "go it alone." No one of us has the expertise, the knowledge, the science, the vision needed to move effectively toward positioning ourselves in a new world and a re-newing ecclesial communion.

I recall that moment in the preparatory work for the Futureshop when meeting with the members of the national office of the Sister Formation Conference in Washington, I asked what amount of conference in-put I would be responsible for presenting (with the not unusual clerical assumption of being "paratus ad omnia"). I was told, however, that my chief contribution would be to listen, and out of that listening experience to share. The situation was expressed quite succinctly: "For nearly two thousand years we women Religious have been listening to you men. It is time we speak for ourselves and you listen." For me, the richest experience of the Futureshop proved to be just that.

I listened with ever deepening appreciation as speaker after speaker — all women Religious — presented their rich insight, personal conviction and purposeful challenge. The small group dialogues, the heart of the program, enabled all the participants to become alternately sharers and receivers.

In this context I was invited to share some of my own convictions about the present state of Religious life, the renewal process, and options for the future. My studies and ministry for so many Religious institutes throughout the world have led me to one immediate conclusion. If we were asked what group of Church personnel has understood best the call of the Council to reform and renewal and responded more readily and completely, there is no doubt in my mind but that it would be the Religious. Religious have given an alert, responsible, creative and dynamic response, not only in followthrough on specific directives but in picking up the tonalities and nuances of the Council as well. Neither clergy, laity nor episcopate equal this response.

But this is as it should be. Born of the Church, in the Church, for the Church, Religious throughout the Christian centuries — even apart from conciliar decree or church mandate — have been the geiger counter measuring gospel awareness or dissonance among the people of God. At critical junctures in Church history periods of profound transformation, of reform and renewal, were either preceded by or concomitant with the rejuvenation of the religious ideal.

A further point of great importance applies directly to the Church in the United States, although I believe the same is true in much of Europe. While all Religious life is indeed in a period of profound and unalterable transition to newer expressions, to more relevant forms, to redefinition of life and ministry, the leadership in this movement is coming not from the men and clerical Religious, as has most often been the case in the past, but rather from the women Religious. In this we are witnessing a new and significant development. Women Religious continue to manifest a deeper perception of the gospel imperative for our day, a more sensitive concern for the needs of the "poor" of every age and class, a keener ability to read the signs of the times, and a capacity to respond with more daring and vigor than their male counterparts. At the same time the inner motivation of their lives is being more deeply scrutinized, their spiritual value system more carefully re-examined and more aptly re-constructed.

This is not to say that nothing significant has been done by the men Religious nor that men Religious are not renewing — far from it. What I mean is that an even greater degree of awareness, initiative, intensity of concern, imaginative, innovative and daring responses are to be found among the women Religious. This does not mean that all orders of women Religious are in this category. While the majority are, there are notable exceptions. There is still evidence of some fearful, hesitant and even contradictory backward movements.

The Council closed in 1965. The imperative for renewal, *Ecclesiae Sanctae*, was issued in 1966. Now, a good piece down the road since the close of the Council, I believe we can locate all Religious institutes in one of three categories: new beginnings; genuinely renewing institutes; or diminishing congregations. Moreover, while asked to speak about options, I believe it is not the options as such that are significant but what I may call "optionizing" as a process. Successful use of this process depends in turn upon the acceptance of two very fundamental principles: the radicalism of renewal and the totality of change. Flowing through the entire renewal movement and profoundly affecting its outcome is the proper use of the two essential resources: time and talent. Due to the post-war surge in vocations, Religious may have presumed that these resources existed in unlimited supply. Many institutes continued to assign people to fill jobs because "it is our work."

Finally, for each institute a viable future will require the successful endurance of three tests. Is the renewal approach truly integrational? Next, to what degree is the institute willing to re-examine its "presence" in Church and society, question that "presence" and in the light of this discernment re-define its purpose and re-assign its goals? Third, while aspiring toward true community experience, to what degree can the order sustain flexible and diverse expressions of lifestyle? But before proceeding to develop these several facets of the future I would like to reflect for a moment on the present struggle: a renewing Church.

The Response of Religious to the Council

Distanced by a decade from the most significant event in ecclesiastical history in the last four hundred years, we can now analyze more objectively the effects of Vatican II on Church life. The forces unleashed in that moment of pentecostal grace continue to work their way through all levels of the faith experience. Significant, irreversible changes have taken place. A beginning has been made, though much more remains to be done. For many the pace is too slow, the decisions too hesitant, and the dialogical process undeveloped. There is the danger, and signs of a fearful retrenchment can be seen. While there is reason for discouragement in some areas of Church life, in the Religious life the overview is encouraging. I do not believe the positive progressive trends can be reversed. There are several significant reasons for this.

Religious men and women are the only group in the Church who were given a direct mandate with a time-schedule to renew: a command performance. Hopefully, this was prompted by a conviction of the value and necessity of the Religious life experience to the whole faith community. It may also have come from a realization of the overpowering stagnation effect of long-standing unquestioned custom. The hold of tradition and the control of strong-centrist organizational structures in Religious institutes may have needed the goading of a specific mandate. In the pre-Vatican II style Religious were not remarkably innovative or spontaneous. Witness the fact that the first appeal to renew went practically unheeded when twenty-six years ago Pius XII at the first world congress on the Religious life called for an updating of rules and constitutions, a renewal of cloister and (believe it or not), an adaptation of the Religious habit. The more recent conciliar exhortation, however, was accepted vigorously. What has happened since '66, especially in institutes of women Religious, is nothing less than phenomenal, as I have indicated above.

Fortunately, many of the major Religious orders in the United States have dropped the terms "experiment" and "experimentation," and have moved to the more enriching as well as more demanding concepts of process development with on-going evaluation techniques to gauge present and past policies and practices while continuing to explore new ideas. No area has been left untouched — from recruitment to retirement, to government, formation, prayer life, spirituality, etc. Permanent offices of research and planning have been developed.

Religious life, a dramatic reliving of the paschal mystery not only for individuals but for entire congregations, manifests an amazing capacity for suffering and dying and being born again. While we have been shaken by many unprecedented phenomena, such as the long exodus since 1966, we are likewise exhilarated by so many new approaches and entirely new beginnings. Moreover, the efforts at renewal are not confined to one congregation or another. It is a universal response. It is as if the entire Religious population of the world formed an enormous thinktank. Formerly, renewal movements depended for the most part upon one or another charismatic leader as a Teresa of Avila or a John of the Cross, an Elizabeth Ann Seton or a Vincent de Paul. Today the movement is cross-cultural and multi-national, calling forth hosts of leaders and collaborators in a truly communal and interdisciplinary response to the complex situation. The future is promising. This is particularly evident in the potential for change and development contained in the hope of full, equal and free participation of women (Religious and lay) in the decision-making processes and the ministries of the Church, local and universal.

Opting and Optionizing

I have been asked to speak of options for the future. I respond by saying "optionizing" as a process is more important.

Some clarifications are needed here. It is necessary to distinguish "option" and "opting" from what I call "optionizing." An option is one of many alternatives that may be chosen. Opting is to select from among the options. Optionizing is neither the option nor the opting. It is rather the very experiencing of the multiplicity of possibilities in the resolution of a given problem. It is the willingness to seek and to explore these multiple possibilities, the encouragement we give to others to discover and to present the variables, even though seemingly contradictory; the openness each manifests to new ideas, the willingness to change personal opinion and attitude. This is an incomparable value. It is a listening to the Spirit. It is dialogical, par excellence. It is reverence for the vision of others that in the end may be far more significant than "my" previously tenaciously held view which increasingly proves to be quite myopic.

If the process toward opting is improper, faulty or erroneous, the final option may be improper, faulty or even downright stupid. Optionizing in the sense above means that given a particular situation we desire to search out and review multiple solutions and their consequences. We totally avoid at this stage of the process a right and wrong stance, a good guys vs. bad guys decision; we preclude a win-lose situation; we prevent a forced yes-no vote; we avoid division. So very often our vote is neither yes nor no but right in between. Optionizing expands the "in-between" to unfold all the richness of thought and possibility it may contain.

There is a further significant value to this procedure — a true spiritual value (or rather, a more directly spiritual value). By the process of optionizing we seek to listen attentively to the voice of the Spirit in each of our members with reverence and respect.

This process has three valuable consequences. These relate to the content and the quality of the final decisions; the agreement or consensus level achieved; and the possibilities for implementation. When a group accepts the process, explores and reviews in an open and welcome spirit the multiplicity of probable answers, the resolution usually will be found in a combination of sev-

eral partially satisfactory responses. The very content, the quality
of the conclusion is constantly improved. Moreover as the exploration for options continues a gradual and increasing consensus
begins to form. Finally, the possibility of implementation follows
upon the degree to which the members commit themselves to a
solution. This commitment will be in proportion to the freedom
of in-put, the caliber of participation, and the understanding of
consequences.

The Three Categories of Religious Institutes

At the beginning of this essay I stated that all Religious communities belong to one of three categories: new, renewing or diminishing. It is time to address these groups directly. Let us speak here
of the second. Hopefully, but by no means certainly, the majority
of orders and congregations seek to identify themselves in the second category: among the genuinely renewing. But the question is
not merely whether or not the renewal chapters have been conducted and the rule re-written. This has been done in most institutes and still the future can remain increasingly dubious. The
question is really one of a deep interior renewal of spirit and an
effective restructuralization of authority. A Religious community
may have produced magnificent documents — accurate, scriptur-
ally sound, theologically brilliant — but these will remain mere
rhetoric, devoid of life, if implementation is barren. Nor is renewal a question of numbers. Many of the smaller orders have manifested singularly impressive resurgence. The key is in three factors: commitment, conviction, and consecration.

Commitment to one's community. Conviction of its worth.
Consecration to its ideals and goals.

It is a question of coping, coping with change, tension, diversity. It is a process of reformation and re-education. It is the ability to develop systems of on-going adaptation and interior renewal. It is not easy to determine if an institute belongs to this
category of the genuinely renewing. Its state will be clearer as we
speak of the first category, the new beginnings, and of the third,
diminishing communities.

This first category is comprised of a surprisingly large number
of new beginnings. We have not as yet accurately determined the
exact number, but CARA has begun this research. Presently, we

estimate that the number of new beginnings are between 150 and 200. These beginnings are of three kinds. The first is comprised of groups of Religious who have left their institutes for a variety of reasons. These reasons usually relate to a dispute on the very meaning of Religious life and the interpretation of the conciliar and post-conciliar documents. Often the root cause is a frustration at the pace or the forced limitations and interpretations of renewal.

It is a very sad phenomenon to separate from one's first allegiance. For the Religious involved it is a trying and traumatic experience. It is a crucifixion, involving family and closest friends. Definitive separation is always the last, the final step in a long process at reconciliation that ultimately fails. In my experience the failure is often a failure to "optionize," as described above. Fortunately the Holy See, through the Congregation of Religious, will uphold the right of the Religious to their vocation in this trying circumstance and, after examination, provide the means by which the new group can begin again in a separate and distinct existence.

The second type of new beginnings is comprised of those Religious who have separated individually from their communities but still desire in some way to continue a Religious life experience. When we reflect on the great number of Religious who have swelled the ranks of the departees — some 27,000 women Religious alone in the last eight years — we are anxious to know more about them, their lives, their hopes, their relationship to the Church. They form a vast potential, not yet sufficiently understood or explored for the sake of the gospel, for the good of the Church.

In the third type of this first category, new beginnings, we discover really original and different approaches. These are comprised of people who have had, for the most part, no previous experience of Religious life as we have known it. There are no set patterns other than an emphasis on communal life and gospel sharing. Comprised of young and older people, of men and women often sharing the same residence, of married couples and celibate members, they are searching for a new response to their inner conviction to live the gospel. While some may be open to greater relationship to the official Church, others have no desire to be acknowledged or recognized "canonically," but want to live simply as men and women of the gospel. Our responsibility is to be open to what the Spirit may be saying through them to us but above all to themselves for their own persons and the good of the people of God.

The third category of Religious communities today is large and challenging. It is an unprecedented phenomenon. To this category belong those communities whose future is very uncertain. They are diminshing; many are facing the completion of their corporate purposes as a Religious institute. Their life is ebbing. Very little attention has been given to this new situation. It is grave and more widespread than we imagine. Surrounding almost every large metropolitan area of the country, there are a number of diminishing or near diminished communities. They have suffered serious losses; they have not been able to attract and retain new members for a decade or more; their median age is constantly rising; their apostolic resources are drained; their financial resources in many instances are precarious; their spirit is at breaking point.

The Religious in this category deserve our greatest support and encouragement. They have given their lives to the Church and its mission. Further study needs to be given to this serious problem. It is an area of research we have only begun to investigate. Optionizing is important here. Every possible solution needs to be explored. One possible solution may be the combination of resources of several communities and the eventual amalgamation of these communities into a new institute. This is not the place to explore this concept in detail, but it does deserve very close attention.

Two Fundamental Principles

Whether an institute is in the first, second, or third category, the factors determining its future will be based upon the acceptance of two fundamental principles: the radicalism of renewal and the totality of change. Here I am proceeding on the assumption that renewal and reform are regarded as imperative, an assumption not universally accepted even in Religious life circles. If this assumption is valid, as it is for the entire Church, then the renewal will be radical. Let us not be afraid of the term. It is precise. It will be radical not in the popular sense of wild and irrational but in the very original meaning of the word — "at the root." We are speaking of root changes. It is not a question of buttressing old structures but of creating new.

Our work is so difficult because there are no "givens," no fixed, set formulae, no neat and clean patterns. We must ask ultimate questions. It is not a question of the style of community life but rather what community is all about. It is not a new interpretation of the obedience-authority relationship but a question of mature human freedom. It is not a question of work but of the essence of ministry. It is not a question of decision but of decision-making.

These questions are not susceptible to simple, direct solutions. Nor can they be imposed, unilateral conclusions. They require research, reflection, cooperative effort. They require a willingness to live with ambiguity, to live with a lack of certitude. But until an institute recognizes the radicalism of the renewal process, these basic, root questions (while there) will simply be avoided or treated as non-questions in the vague hope that with time they will disappear. However, not only will they not go away, we may dim the vision of our prophets, silence their voices, and the "now-time" will pass away.

Once we begin to discern and to confront the hard questions, the validity of the second principle emerges: the totality of change. Despite the encouraging exhortation of Cardinal Newman so often quoted today calling our attention to the necessary and unavoidable nexus between growth and change, change for all of us still comes hard. If this is so in ordinary times, the truly revolutionary conditions of today have rendered change for many communities nothing less than traumatic and destructive. We have made sacred what in itself is not holy and now are burdened with guilt over changing our sacral self-creations. So dependent had we become upon the unexamined past that the suddenness of a present-future completely overwhelmed us.

Our efforts to piece things together frequently increased frustration because we were doing just that — patchwork. A good example of this is what occurred in many communities (and is still present in some). Convinced that the formation of Religious is the key issue, a community sets itself toward a radical reorganization of its formation program, from pre-entrance to post-profession, only to find out it is not workable because the rest of the community is nowhere ready for it. Forced into an unchanged context of community life and custom, it creates as many problems as it attempted to resolve. But in doing this it may serve a dual purpose. Providing the community is open to the truth of the situation, and the formation people can sustain the agony, a gradual re-organization of the whole life can take place. With great difficulty a community begins to realize the issue is not formation, it is not administration and authority, it is not community, it is not prayer — it is an entire new way of thinking and feeling and doing. It is a radical shift from a closed to an open system with implications beyond our expectation that require a total approach. Many communities have not yet realized how sweeping, how wholistic is the requirement of the Council.

The very decree, *Perfectae Caritatis*, is all too easily read, even by some who make unique claims about it. There we are directed to re-examine our entire manner of living together, of praying together, of working together, of governing and of being governed and — here is the crunch — to bring all this into accord with the changed conditions of our times, the needs of the Church and the requirements of a given culture. This itself is a gigantic task, an enormous demand. To it we must add the further and singularly significant directive: namely, that all the above is to be accomplished in view of the sociological, the psychological, as well as the economic needs of the Religious themselves as distinct persons in a total society, ecclesial and civic.

The change is total. These directives require adjustment in the entire system. Nor can our effort be a one-shot deal: "We had our renewal chapter, now let's get back to normal." And equally important, even if all the above becomes the constant concern of our community, we may be very faulty in the way we go about implementing our concern. Inside and outside the institute, the methodology we are to employ requires changes that by themselves, for many Religious, are as disturbing and perhaps more disconcerting than intrinsic changes.

Inside — the maximal feasible participation (MFP) of the total membership is to be a constant goal. This makes new and continuous demands on each unit of the organization, as well as upon each individual member.

Outside — we need to engage the expert. With insight and humility we must apply the tremendous advances in the sacred and humane sciences, theological and scriptural — as well as the sociological, psychological and administrative sciences — to the task at hand.

Ten years down the road, we are only in the early stages of genuine renewal, effective restructuralization and precise redefinition of Religious life. We have only just begun.

Appendix I

Resource Centers

Reference materials referred to can be obtained from the following Resource Centers:

1. **World Future Society,** 4916 St. Elmo Avenue, Washington, D.C. 20014.

    The Futurist, A Journal of Forecasts, Trends and Ideas about the Future.

    The Educational Significance of the Future: A Report prepared for the U.S. Commissioner of Education, by Harold G. Shane, 1972.

    Educational Futurism: In Pursuance of Survival, by John D. Pullman and Jim R. Bowman, University of Oklahoma press: Norman, 1975.

2. **Community Services Office,** School Sisters of St. Francis, 1501 S. Layton Boulevard, Milwaukee, WI 53215.

    Pages on the Future: Resource Materials prepared for Futures Workshops, by School Sisters of St. Francis, Milwaukee, 1975.

    Futures Workshops: A group of Resource Persons available in teams.

3. **Dialogue House,** 45 West 10 Street, New York, N. Y. 10011.

    2At a Journal Workshop: the Basic Text and Guide for Using the Intensive Journal, Dialogue House Library, 1975.

    Intensive Journal/Process Meditation Workshops and Training Programs for Journal Consultants.

4. **St. Joseph's Abbey,** Spencer, MA 01562

    Simple Method of Contemplative Prayer, tapes by William Menninger, OCSO.

Practical Religious Experience Workshops and Training Sessions for Leaders.

5. **Leadership Conference of Women Religious,** 1330 Massachusetts Avenue, N.W., Washington, D.C. 20005.

   New Visions, New Roles: Women in the Church. Five papers dealing with the relation of women to religion and Religious institutions, 1975. Published by and available from LCWR in Washington, D.C.

   LCWR Resource Kit on Women. Prepared by the Ecclesial Role of Women Committee of the LCWR, 1975. Twelve packets. Available from LCWR Focus on Women, 5350 E. Springfield Road, Rockford, IL 61111.

6. **National Sisters Communication Service,** 1962 S. Shenandoah Street, Los Angeles, CA 90034.

   A Guide to National Organizations of Sisters in the U.S. An up-to-date and accurate listing of national organizations of women Religious.

7. Center for Applied Research in the Apostolate (CARA) 1234 Massachusetts Ave. NW, Washington, D.C. 20005. Documentation Center on materials from renewal programs. Valuable assistance in research in every aspect of Religious life.

Appendix II

Basic Shifts in Emphasis of Value Trends in the 80s

Compiled by Dorothy Cropper, SHCJ

Research Assistant
Sister Formation Conference

On the last day of the Futureshop the participants were asked to brainstorm on the consequences of nine trends that Sister Shawn Madigan, CSJ mentioned in her presentation, "Projected Tomorrows and Effects of Formation Today." The following is the result:

Trend One: There will be increasing stress on the qualitative (better) rather than the quantitative (more) aspects of living.

  Negative effects: Such a stress would lead the "better" to be too selective, indifferent, abstract, segregated and so lead the "more" to despair, introspection, and feelings of neglect by the "elite educated."

  Positive effects: Emphasizing quality brings forth deeper faith and sharing, lifting of burdensome structures, service orientation, and ability to be challenging while remaining supportive.

Trend Two: Growing movement toward interdependence — particularly among the educated — will replace the excessive independence or dependence attitudes of adults.

Negative effects: People will be divided and power groups will emerge such as educated vs. uneducated. A strong fear is that most have not yet experienced independence, and so instead of interdependence either an amorphous mass will result or the overspecialized will rule. Total loss of self-identity will become a strong probability.

Positive effects: Growing awareness of self will in turn lead to development of community awareness which will in turn result in global sharing. Focus on persons leads to fuller realization of the Body of Christ and so the gospel call to ecumenical living will become a reality. Breakdown of hierarchical structure will give birth to a charismatic, supportive community not defined by special proximity.

Trend Three: Being primarily concerned with private need fulfillment will give way to concern for meeting more public needs.

Negative effects: The fear of not being taken care of will cause fragmentation, frustration, and possibly disintegration of community. Talk of public concern will polarize and pressure some people. The "state" would become our religion.

Positive effects: We will be freed to work with a broader vision of Church as world and become so caught up in "other consciousness" that worry about self will disappear. This trend will call forth responsibility, accountability, reexamination of present structures. Concern for public will force us to reevaluate our work and choose where we can best serve. Competition will be reduced and intercommunity collaboration will be strengthened.

Trend Four: Personal self-development and aspirations of members of an organization will take gradual priority over organizational conveniences, order, efficiency, and expenditures for profit.

Negative effects: The worst effects envisioned were inability to take a corporate thrust because so many would be fear-ridden, individualistic, independent, competitive, or filled with tension and discouragement. Insensitivity to others' needs, lack of integration of faith and life, each one doing her own thing, lack of funds for physical and emotional needs would lead to misconception of celibacy, loss of vocation, and finally extinction of religious life.

Positive effects: A refounding of community where leadership will be charismatic rather than appointed is anticipated. Organizations will be more communal, potential will be developed, manipulation of others will give way to interdependent responsibility for each other. Love will flow from life experiences. Enriched personal relationships, greater concern, greater capacity for a celibate life will all result in community becoming more viable witness to the gospel in a pilgrim Church.

Trend Five: Increasing demand for participation is replacing the old authoritarianism or executive power. A growth in anti-authoritarianism will continue, resulting in greater alienation from outmoded institutions and reduction of toleration for any form of self-alienation.

Negative effects: The worst to be realized from this trend would be a leaderless group of common denominators. Lack of leadership and support could result in apathy, loss of membership, collapse of community life, and dissolution of institution. Other fears expressed were that total participation could eventually become a new form of authoritarianism, thus causing a return to structured, centralized power.

Positive effects: A liberation of self will lead to greater toleration of others and shared weaknesses will nourish new strengths in the Lord. New creative communities, cultivating moral and personal development through presence to others' sufferings and recognition of each one's worth, will transform the world. Looseness of structure will enable groups to include marginal persons, become self-directed rather than crisis-oriented, and develop norms for Church and civic government.

Trend Six: Diversity and pluralism will continue to replace uniformity and centralization.

Negative effects: Lack of unity will cause fragmentation, diffusion of energy, loss of corporate identity, and destruction of community life. Fear, despair, loneliness, abnormality, discouragement, activism will diffuse people's energies and destroy their sense of commitment.

Positive effects: Healthier communities calling one another to leadership will produce self-directed persons possessing a sense of personal worth, thus calling forth deeper commitment to a God-centered approach to ministry. Deeper spirituality rooted in faith in Christ and one another will encourage great reverence for diversity of persons as well as profit from communal discernment that will give rise to reconciliation and a fuller revelation of global responsibility.

Trend Seven: *The leisure ethic will receive as much emphasis as the work ethic, with the trend toward a three-day work week increasing until 1980.*

Negative effects: Because leisure activities have never been encouraged or cultivated, persons are ill prepared to cope with free time. Boredom, anxiety, and guilt will ensue. Work can no longer be used as an escape mechanism and people will be forced to face painfully intimate-personal relationships. Space and privacy problems will cause people to structure their leisure as they once structured their work.

Positive effects: There will be a rebirth of contemplative actions that will deepen people's affective spirituality, develop a sharing of self with community, neighborhood, and intimate friends. Emphasis will shift from quantity to quality, from human production to human worth, from giving to sharing. There will be greater reliance on God's power and realization of his gifts of humanity, nature, fine arts, and beauty.

Trend Eight: *The consciousness of growing intimacy needs may see a new flourishing of family life and community life as essential life supports in an ambiguous society. This will replace the prior career satisfaction that was the main support of many people in the past era.*

Negative effects: People could become isolated, self-centered, and non-productive because too much energy will be expended on either wallowing in personal togetherness or in feeling guilty because of inability to develop intimate relationships. Sexual satisfaction, homosexuality, over-dependence on feelings will cause weakening of faith and loss of celibacy. Physical attraction will eventually lead to lack of creativity, freedom, and destruction of personhood.

Positive effects: Tenderness, intimacy, appreciation, trust, support and strength will develop as we grow into a deeper level of friendship. Deeper family and community life will sustain us in painful conflicts and we will interact as wounded healers. Integration of human self with religious self will help us to accept another's role as "being" instead of as "doing." Deep friendships in the Lord will support each in different ministries and new structures will arise to promote Christian love on a global scale.

Trend Nine: Promotion and increased acceptance of change is already replacing the former preservation of status quo for organizational systems.

Negative effects: Increased change will lead to loss of corporate charity, corporate identity and a general sense of direction and stability. Vatican II renewal will cease and technology will replace morality. Since some people will never learn how to cope with change, there will be emotional stress and increase of mental illness.

Positive effects: A refound commonality will call forth new recruits accepting differences, growing in intimacy, interiorizing a spirit of openness, and going forth with a geographic charism to create an intercommunity of open-endedness. In this living Church which will recognize equality of ministries, organizational systems will be revitalized and the Church will be completed in the future gobal village.

Conclusion°

Running through the above comments is a strong element of hope in the future, deep concern for personal worth, and eagerness to build a better dynamic world community. A broader vision of the Church is foreseen in which people will become so caught up in "other consciousness" that worry about self will become a minority concern.

The fear concerns expressed by some should be heard as guidelines for future action. A sensitivity to weaker or more timid persons is so prevalent in all of the above discussions that they should be reassured of strong support in looking to the future.

°(includes all nine trends)

The Contributors

Mary Ann Barnhorn, SNDdeN is Director of a new on-going intercommunity formation program, "An Active Spirituality for the Global Community" in Cincinnati. She is also Director of an Intercommunity Novitiate Program for the Archdiocese of Cincinnati, and Vice-President for the Pastoral Council of the Archdiocese.

Margaret Brennan, IHM is the Major Superior of the Sister Servants of the Immaculate Heart of Monroe, Michigan. She is also a past-president of the Leadership Conference of Women Religious and has been very active in its various programs.

Paul M. Boyle, CP. Father Boyle is the Provincial of Holy Cross Province of the Congregation of the Cross, Passionists. He is a past-president of the Conference of Major Superiors of Men, and has also served as consultant to a variety of religious congregations on canonical and financial affairs.

Bernadette Casey, RSM did graduate work at the University of Duquesne's Institute of Man to prepare for her work in Initial Formation. She is Formation Director for the Sisters of Mercy in Providence, Rhode Island.

James Connor, SJ is working as a Research Associate at the Jesuit Conference of Major Superiors, Washington, D.C. He is the former Provincial of the Maryland Province of Jesuits.

Colman Coogan, FSC is the present Provincial of the Maryland Province of Christian Brothers.

Shawn M. Copeland, OP serves as Executive Director for the National Black Sisters Conference, and is also a published poet, writer, and lecturer. Presently, she is a member of the Steering Committee for the 41st International Congress, and is on the Board of Directors of the Catholic Committee on Urban Ministry in Pittsburgh.

Louise Dempsey, CSJ is President of the Sisters of St. Joseph of Peace whose headquarters are located in Washington, D.C. She is LCWR's representative on the Bicentennial Commission and was also an active member of the U.S. Center for International Women's Year Advisory Committee.

Margaret Ebbing, SC is the Assistant Administrator for East Coast Migrant Health Projects. Nursing and Health Education have been her primary interests and life-long work. Most recently, she was Administrator of a hospital in Africa.

Maria Gatza, IHM is serving as an Assistant to the General Superior of the Sisters, Servants of the Immaculate Heart of Mary, Monroe, Michigan. She has previously served on such community committees as Formation, Spiritual Renewal, and Education.

Mary Gehring, OCD is a member of the Barrington, Rhode Island Carmelite Monastery. She has been active in both the Association of Contemplative Sisters and the Carmelite Communities Association.

Ann Gormly, SNDdeN is Assistant to the Executive Director of U.S. Catholic Mission Council in Washington, D.C. She earned a PhD in Spanish at Catholic University; served as Dean of Students at Trinity College; and was Director of Apostolic Services for the Maryland Province of the Sisters of Notre Dame de Namur.

Karen Gosser, SHCJ has been Coordinator of the Ecumenical Center for Urban Education in Portland, Oregon. Her research there resulted in the publication of a resource guide for local churches, "Women, Church, Change." She is now Religion Instructor at St. Leonard's Academy in Philadelphia, and is editing a community newsletter on peace and justice issues.

Doris Gottemoeller, RSM is presently serving as Assistant Administrator General of the Sisters of Mercy of Bethesda, MD, and is also a doctoral student in Theology at Fordham University. She has published articles and reviews in *Sisters Today* and *Review for Religious*.

Marlene Halpin, OP holds a doctorate in Philosophy from Catholic University and is Coordinator of Continuing Education and Professor of Philosophy at the Aquinas Institute of Theology in Dubuque. She is doing extensive work in designing programs for priests and Religious.

Ann Heilman, SFCC is Assistant Professor of Psychology at Loyola University in Chicago. She has her doctorate in Clinical Psychology from Ohio State, and has a private clinical practice. She has been a consultant to several formation teams.

Maria Iglesias, SC is a part-time Parish Worker in a South Bronx neighborhood. As a student, and later as a graduate of the Mexican American Cultural Center in Texas, she coordinated programs for the Spanish Speaking. She was elected Chairperson of Sisters Uniting, and is a member of the coordinating team of Las Hermanas.

Vincentia Joseph, MSBT is an Assistant Professor in the School of Social Service at Catholic University. She holds a PhD in Social Work from Catholic University and is Project Director of the Parish Social Service-Action Program. She is also consultant to several Diocesan Catholic Charities on the development of Parish Social Ministry Programs.

Kathleen Keating, SSJ is a member of the Sisters of St. Joseph of Holyoke, Mass. Presently she is serving as the Chairperson of the National Assembly of Women Religious, Chicago, Illinois.

Nancy McAuley, RSCJ is Documentation Supervisor at CARA in Washington, D.C. She has a doctorate from the International University in California, and has specialized in communication and related fields. Before joining CARA, she had been Director of the Social Research Committee of the Archdiocese of St. Louis.

Ruth McGoldrick, SP has been the Executive Director of Sister Formation Conference in Washington, D.C. since 1973. Before assuming the directorship, she had served her own Community as Vocation Director, Novice Director, and Formation Coordinator. She holds a MRE in Spirituality from St. Mary's, Indiana, and has taught Spiritual Theology in Intercommunity and College Formation Programs. She has been a consultant for numerous renewal programs, and is presently a board member of several organizations of women Religious.

Shawn Madigan, CSJ is presently a doctoral candidate in Theology at Catholic University. She teaches a summer course at Fontbonne College on "Futurology and Theology," and is also working on her Congregation's Secretariat for the Future.

Rhonda Meister, SP is a Social Worker at Mercy Hospital in Springfield, MA. She is actively engaged in working with youth and social justice groups, and is also currently a member of her Community's Representative Assembly and Vocation Committee.

Margaret M. Modde, OSF is presently a student of Canon Law at Catholic University. She is the former Director of the National Sisters Vocation Conference, a post which she held since the opening of the national office in 1970. She and Dr. John Koval directed the NSVC research project on "Women Who Have Left Religious Life."

Vilma Seelaus, OCD is the Formation Director of the Barrington Carmel in Rhode Island. Besides publishing numerous articles in contemplative periodicals, she has worked to form the Association of Contemplative Sisters, and has served two terms as president of the association.

Alice St. Hilaire, SP holds a doctorate in Philosophy from St. Louis University. She has taught Philosophy at Seattle University and at St. Thomas Seminary College, and has served for several years on her own community's formation team. She is now the Director of the Retirement Program for the Sacred Heart Province of her order.

Nancy Swift, RCE is Assistant Professor of Religion and Religious Education at Catholic University. She holds an ME from Boston College in Clinical Psychology; an MA in Liturgy from Notre Dame; and a PhD in Liturgy from Strasbourg, France. She is also Consultant to the American Council of her Congregation.

Kathleen Uhler, OSF is a doctoral graduate of Georgetown University, and is now a faculty member in the Philosophy Department. She directs summer workshops on Religious Life for her congregation in which she develops a theme of adapting phenomenological analysis to a search for the roots of Religious commitment.

Cassian Yuhaus, CP. Father Yuhaus holds a doctorate in Ecclesiology from the Pontifical University in Rome. He has done postgraduate work at Fordham, Munich, Laval, and Montreal universities. He was a professor in the theologate and Director of Seminarians for his order, and has served as Assistant to the Provincial and as Provincial Consultor, as well as President of the International Commission on the Charism of the Passionist Congregation and the Meaning of Religious Life. Presently, he is Director of the Religious Life Department at CARA in Washington, D.C. Father is the Founder of the International Institute for Religious Life. He has published many works, both in the area of spirituality and of research on Religious Life.